THE STORY OF YOUR DOG

THE STORY
OF YOUR DOG

A Straightforward Guide to a
Complicated Animal

Learn the surprising connections between your unique dog's
breed, behaviors, evolution, and genetics to communicate
better, train easier, and build a lasting bond

Brandon McMillan

HarperOne
An Imprint of HarperCollinsPublishers

HarperCollins books may be purchased for educational, business, or sales promotional use. For information, please email the Special Markets Department at SPsales@harpercollins.com.

FIRST HARPERCOLLINS PAPERBACK EDITION PUBLISHED IN 2023

Designed by Kyle O'Brien

Library of Congress Cataloging-in-Publication Data is available upon request.

ISBN 978-0-06-304065-6

23 24 25 26 27 LBC 5 4 3 2 1

To my late brother Brian.
I miss you every day.

CONTENTS

INTRODUCTION:
WHAT'S THE STORY OF YOUR DOG?

I was a teenager the first time I saw a rookie border collie at a herding ranch. This dog was six months old and had never seen sheep in her life. She was completely untrained and naive to the world—but the minute she caught sight of the flock, her body stiffened, her head dropped, her ears flattened, and her entire frame leaned with attention as she went into full stalking mode. Zeroed in on the animals, she burst into action, charging at the flock, running circles around them, and nipping at their heels. In under a minute, fifteen meandering sheep became a tight, compact group, ready to be safely penned up for the night.

My jaw dropped. I asked the ranch owner how the pup could possibly know what to do without any training. She looked at me and then at the dog—now looking every inch a puppy again, with one ear up, one ear down, and her whole body twitching with excitement as she watched over "her" sheep. The owner shrugged and said simply, "They were wolves."

Of course that was only half the story. Wolves aren't known for their sheepherding. The rest happened in the thousands of years that passed between ancient wolves and that modern-day border collie—an evolutionary process that may be unequaled by any other creature. The wolf became domesticated by and bonded to humans, then underwent a long, slow, definitive transformation from all-purpose omnivore to the perfect dog for herding sheep.

What I witnessed that day shifted my entire perspective on dogs, and over the years, I became a more accomplished animal trainer because of it. I realized that the primal drives each animal carries within are critical components in our human understanding of dog behavior and what compels those behaviors in the first place.

On a hypothetical level, we all know dogs are descended from wolves. Of course they are. But few of us take that fact into account when we look at our own dogs. More often than not, we imagine them kind of like furry children—projecting simplified versions of our own logic and emotions onto them. When they bolt out of the yard, we think they're being naughty, rather than following their instincts to seek prey. When they get snippy around the food bowl, we call it aggression, rather than a defense tactic. When they maniacally race around the house or go crazy on a toy, we say they're being playful, rather than striving to fulfill their genetic impulse to exhaust each day's mountain of energy. When they pee on the floor after an hour alone, we think they're spiteful, rather than the truth–they are so stressed at being separated from their pack they can hardly stand it.

And this is just the beginning of the miscommunications and misunderstandings between humans and dogs. The critical fact we tend to forget is that fifteen thousand years of genetics factor into every move our dogs make. Every issue, personality trait, and quirky habit of our domestic dogs is rooted in links to their ancestors and the ensuing centuries of domestication and job-specific breeding.

History shaped domestic dogs and then their breeds, coaxing their behavior away from wildness, shyness, and the other survival, territorial, and mating instincts of wolves. Humans set out to make wolves cooperative, and eventually worked to recast them as specialized dogs, experts at valued jobs like guarding, herding, and hunting. It worked. Over time, we created hundreds of different breeds capable of doing highly specific, useful jobs for us.

Fast-forward to the twenty-first century, when less than 5 percent of dogs have ever even had an obedience class. Only a minuscule portion of them work, doing jobs they were designed to do. Many of those tasks are obsolete now anyway. Instead, today's pet dogs are lounging on the couch, snoozing in the bed, chasing their tails in the backyard, bounding after tennis balls, or romping in the dog park. They're bringing laughter and companionship and love to our lives. At least the lucky ones are. The not so fortunate—dogs I see all the time as part of my work—are huddled in cages at animal shelters, not knowing their lives are at stake or why. Far too often the reasons go right back to their wolf origins and their job-specific breeding. Dogs are abandoned because they're too energetic or too aloof, too aggressive or too defensive, or even because they get too lonely, whiny, and dependent.

To say the fate of both "naughty" dogs and shelter dogs who end up in trouble is not their fault is an epic understatement. Humans spent thousands of years selecting and shaping these creatures to behave a certain way. Now that we don't need—or even like—some of those traits anymore, there's no easy way to turn them off.

Case in point: several years ago, I took my Jack Russell terrier out for a quiet morning at a dog-friendly park. I picked a sunny spot, spread a blanket, stretched out, and opened a book. My dog Pepe (more about him in Chapter 7) took off to engage in his favorite sport: squirrel chasing. He had caught plenty of rats, but squirrels were his pipe dream—the ones that always got away. Everything was right with the world until I caught sight of an idyllic scene unfolding about thirty yards away. A little girl, five or six years old, was slowly, gently reaching her little hand toward a fat squirrel to offer him a peanut. She set it on the ground beside her foot, and the squirrel calculated the risk and stepped in to grab it. He scurried a few feet up a tree trunk and proceeded to eat the peanut while the kid watched and laughed. Her parents looked on, smiling. Heck, it was so sweet I smiled, too—until I caught a glimpse of Pepe, maybe twenty feet from this family, his attention fixated on that squirrel.

It happened fast. The girl offered another peanut, the squirrel edged her way, Pepe saw his chance, and he took off like a shot. As the child, her family, and a few other folks who had been enjoying the peaceful morning looked on, Pepe sank his teeth into the poor distracted rodent, then gave it a giant shake that surely broke its neck and killed it instantly. The girl screamed, the father shouted, the mom went running toward Pepe, but he was not quite done. As we all looked on in horror, he braced the squirrel's body with his right front paw, decapitated it in one swift motion, trotted over to me with the head in his mouth, and dropped it at my feet.

All eyes turned to me then, father of the monster.

Trust me when I tell you there is no etiquette that works in that moment—no suitable gesture or polite words that can make it right. Logic and history told me my dog had acted on an instinct as primal and deep as the urge to eat or to mate, something honed in his breed until it was sharp and undeniable, but that was not the moment to explain such a thing to a crying child or a bunch of disgusted onlookers. Instead, I scooped up dog, book, and blanket, and started what felt like a miles-long walk of shame to the car. For his part, Pepe had at last caught his white whale, and he held his head high.

It would be a long time before we'd dare show our faces at that park again!

Just a hundred years ago, Pepe would have been a rock star on a farm, in a shop, or on a feed lot. His focus on his quarry would have been an asset, and his fast, brutal execution style would have been a source of his owner's pride. He would have a lifelong job, and he'd likely have been bred in hopes of creating more small, deadly hunters to follow in his footsteps.

The breed's drives and actions haven't changed in the last century. All that is different is our perception of them.

———

My guess is that you're reading this book because you, too, have felt like the owner of a little monster when your dog behaves in certain alarming, disturbing, or curious ways. Maybe you've tried to train those behaviors away and are hitting a wall. Maybe you don't know where to start with training and are already more than a little frustrated. Maybe you're feeling exhausted by living with a dog you don't understand. Maybe you don't even own a dog yet and are hoping to learn a bit about what you're in for.

Regardless of what brought you here—I'm glad you picked up this book. In my decades of working with dogs and humans, I've found it is the information in these pages that separates the struggling owners from the ones bonded with, and inseparable from, their dogs.

Your dog has primal instincts that have absolutely nothing to do with you. And like Pepe, your dog likely has a long and deliberate line of purpose-driven breeding in its history.

The reason this all matters is the same one that made that moment at the herding ranch a game changer for me. Understanding your dog—the story of your dog—in terms of both genetic history and environmental development makes you a better owner, better trainer, and better companion. If you use that knowledge to influence your dog's behavior, it can make him or her a better pet, too. The bond between you and your dog will grow and deepen from there.

In the last ten years of my career I've really changed my mindset on training. I used to try and please all my clients by proving a point and solving their dog's issues no matter what. Sometimes this was accomplished with aversive methods that I look back on and regret. I didn't know then what I know now. Once I learned the history of dog breeds and understood their origins, that knowledge gave me a new perspective for training.

I realized the futility of trying to cancel out behavior that's ingrained into DNA. With this in mind, I learned to meet dogs in the middle and train according to their specific genetics. Nowadays when a client wants me to solve an issue that I know goes against the dog's natural, genetic instincts, I just say no. I explain the history of their dog, and we talk about how that history informs the dog's drives. Psychological drives are deep, instinctive pulls that help creatures and species survive—things like the drive to find food, the drive to mate, and the drive to nurture and protect their young. There's an added wrinkle in the concept of drive when it comes to dogs, because humans have been tamping down certain drives in certain dogs for centuries (sometimes longer), and we've been heightening and strengthening other drives at the same time. We've created dogs who are born with powerful drives to hunt by sight or scent, to herd, to protect, to retrieve.

Once my clients understand where their dogs are coming from and why, then we can put our heads together to find ways to let these dogs be true to their nature that is comfortable for everyone involved.

When you look at your dog, no matter what breed (and if you don't know your dog's breed or breeds, there are ways to find out—see Appendix B for more information), the vestiges of wolves are still there. The traits that evolved to help your dog survive a particular climate or geography or resource challenge are still there. The residue of the work its ancestors did is still there. The choices breeders made over centuries to influence appearance and temperament and ability are still there. The purposes for those adaptations may have waned, but remnants of the traits remain.

But no matter what kind of dog you have, no matter how old or young or well trained or well-bred, your beloved companion is strongly influenced by his or her DNA. The result of these genetic distinctions shows up in every inch and action—from the size and shape of a dog's head (and the brain inside it) to the length and curve of his tail, from the texture of her fur to the webbing (or lack of webbing) between her toes. It's in their lung capacity, their tolerance for heat and cold, their appetites for food and exercise, and whether and how they bark. It goes beyond their structure and deep into their psychological profiles.

Perhaps you're lucky enough to have a dog with more than a few breeds mixed in. Throughout this book I'm going to break down breeds and dog groups, but keep in mind that this structure is meant *especially* for readers with dogs that exhibit multiple breeds. The investigative work of reading about the many dog groups and recognizing those behaviors in your dog is the key to understanding the wonderfully complicated animal in front of you.

———

After fifteen thousand years, it's time we put our dogs' genetics in perspective and learn how to work *with* them instead of against them, and that's what I set out to do with this book. Part 1 looks at where it all began—the domestication of wolves, how people have adapted their looks and personalities and behavioral traits ever since, and why those traits sometimes present in unfortunate ways for the modern dog owner. In Part 2, we'll take things a step further and look at each of the major breed groups (and of course mixed breeds) to get at the heart of common genetically based behavior issues and exactly what you can do about them. Most importantly, I'll discuss how you can work *with* your dog's unique genetic quirks and drives instead of constantly having to push back against them.

One word of caution: I use breeds and dog groups to organize this book, but that isn't an endorsement for the American Kennel Club. The key to being a great dog owner isn't how much money you spent on your dog or what its perfect features are or how closely it aligns with one of the breeds we're going to cover in Part 2—it's your dedication to understanding what drives your unique pup.

Lastly, I want to thank you for picking up this book and for your commitment to your dog. Dogs have evolved to have relationships with humans—it's as natural as eating and sleeping for them. It's in their DNA. But as you may be starting to understand, behavior problems are also in your dog's DNA—things like chewing, high energy, territorial barking, chasing the cat. This can make for a hot and cold experience for dog owners who feel ignored and disrespected by dogs that have evolved to communicate with them but don't listen, respond, or behave. So how do you break through to your dog and make communication a two-way street? This is where bonding becomes important. Bonding with your dog is what this book is all about—it starts with the decision to know what motivates your unique dog, and then to lean into your dog's DNA, understanding them on a genetic level. I promise you there's a strong bond with your dog on the other side of that process. At the very least, you'll finally learn what drives the animal sharing your home with you.

I've been training animals my entire life, and along the way I've heard countless tips and theories about how to do it best. Through all these years, one guiding statement about the psyches of dogs stands out above the rest. To really understand where a dog is coming from, you have to start by acknowledging the bedrock truth of the species: *Once, they were wolves.*

PART ONE

WHAT DRIVES A DOG

FROM A WOLF

When you grow up in a circus family, working with animals feels like a birthright. All the most important adults of my childhood were animal trainers—and the kids naturally followed in their footsteps. As a toddler, I snuggled and bottle-fed tiger cubs. As a preschooler, I rode elephants, chatted with bears, cleaned up after monkeys, and handled snakes like it was all the normal, everyday business of a four-year-old. As a young boy, I studied the ways my dad and my uncle moved when they worked the big cats, mimicking how their feet practically danced through the enclosure—always on their toes, ready to react.

It was a nomadic, strange, and sometimes lonely life for a kid, but it was never dull.

In time, with total immersion and plenty of opportunities to practice, I picked up the skills of the family business. I learned to train animals of all sizes and temperaments, to respect them, to read their body language, to know when to push for a little more trust or cooperation and when to call it a day. I learned to move deliberately, knowing the animals were reading my body language, too. By the time I was ten I could do a fair job of working with most species, but the ones that were my closest allies, my playmates, and even my private source of pocket money were dogs.

I had a knack for training them, so much so that by around the third grade I'd figured out I could use my skills to do private training for the residents of whatever town we were living in (and there were a lot of them). I made up a few hand-colored flyers, but the bread and butter of my business was to catch a dog in the act of misbehaving—jumping up on people, not coming when called, counter surfing, being destructive or aggressive to other dogs, or just not responding in general. If I saw a dog had a behavior issue, then I knew I could help. I'd march up to the person at the other end of the leash (or the front door if I spotted the dog in the yard) and offer to help—for a small fee. Most people were so surprised at my confidence-to-size ratio that they would give me a shot. And so I made canine friends and left behind better-trained dogs pretty much wherever I went.

When I got a little older, the excitement and the bigger jobs that came with working large, exotic animals caught my attention, and I traveled to every continent except Antarctica, and of course to Hollywood, honing my skills and training wildlife for television shows, movies, commercials, and music videos. I built a foundation of knowledge and experience that qualified me to train just about any living creature, from the colossal elephant to the mighty wolf to the lowly cockroach. Ultimately, though, after working within earshot of a high-kill animal shelter in Southern California, I realized that the animals I most wanted to work with were the dogs barking in those kennels. I had been scoping out dogs' behavior problems and helping to resolve them since I was a kid. For those dogs the stakes were sky-high—nothing less than life and death. It was impossible to ignore them.

The way I gravitated toward dogs, the choice I made to follow that inclination and make their rescues and forever-home placements my life's work, was an organic, easy decision. I get dogs. I feel a natural affinity with them, a simple joy in their company, and an overwhelming impulse to protect them when they're misunderstood or mistreated.

That connection isn't unique to me, and it didn't just happen overnight or even over my lifetime. For thousands of years, the bonds between humans and canines have been forming and deepening. Our species rely on each other, and even as the range of appearances, temperaments, and skills of dog breeds widens, in many ways we're still living the outcomes of the time when ancient humans and dogs' oldest ancestors—wolves—first forged a tenuous partnership. We still have work to do. And we still have issues, big ones.

The heart of those issues is this: my Chihuahua, your Lab, your neighbor's beagle, and every other pet dog we know have the vestiges of wolf DNA coursing through their veins. Those genes account for some of the behaviors that most frequently cause tension between dogs and owners—things like shyness, aggression, and territoriality. Such issues can all too easily end with dogs being abandoned in shelters, and owners at a loss to define what went wrong except to say their pets were wild or untrainable. (I have a special place in my heart for dogs who fall into that last category—and a list that stretches around the block of "untrainable" dogs I've brought home, taught basic and advanced obedience, and placed with forever families who love them to pieces.) If we want to truly understand our dogs, train them effectively, and keep genetic behaviors from eroding our relationships with them, we owe it to them to set aside our anthropomorphism and take a close look at the primitive drives that are an indelible part of their minds and hearts.

Once Upon a Time

Thousands of years ago, on a cold hillside in what's now China or Mongolia, Germany or Ireland, an ancient hunter makes his way through dense brush, tracking the movements of a wolf. The ancient man is a hunter-gatherer—the only means of self-preservation available to him at this point in history. He ekes out his survival one day at a time. The wolf is a wild creature with no loyalties but to its own pack. The man has seen the wolf's gift for scenting and tracking prey, and so tracking the wolf helps him find potential food sources. The wolf in turn may have picked up a few meals of scraps hanging around the man's shelter. The two have learned to tolerate each other (at least most of the time), but they're not friends . . . yet.

Fast-forward to today, to a major airport in New York or London, Tel Aviv or Beijing. A dog wearing a vest with government insignia and an expression of total focus threads a path through dozens of luggage racks, stopping and starting, putting its nose to the ground and then in the air, searching for contraband. Close behind him, a handler follows, noting the dog's movements, monitoring distractions, watching for an alert that will let her know the substance they're "hunting" has been found.

At first glance, the two scenes are mirrors of each other, millennia apart. But what happens at the end of the day shows how different they are. The wolf and prehistoric man go their separate ways—the wolf slinking silently home to its pack under a rocky ledge in the woods; the man cautiously making his way back to a family and a fire and a crude shelter. They keep tabs on each other, but they don't let their guard down or get too close. At best, there's a grudging respect between them because their shared interests may help them survive.

When the drug-sniffing dog of today finds contraband, the handler immediately offers a reward—playtime with a favorite toy. Later, the dog's body language is open and eager as the partners hop in a truck together for the ride home. The handler feeds the dog, then spends time showering him with affection and praise. When she tucks him into his kennel for the night, the dog curls up contentedly, tired and satisfied. The two are partners who understand each other, and, most important, it is tacitly understood by both that they are members of the same pack.

That's quite an evolutionary turn—from separate animals living separate lives to members of the same pack, happily relying on each other. This relationship, one that slowly and surely evolved out of the tenuous connection between early humans and wolves, is one of the longest and most cooperative interspecies partnerships in all of history. While there's endless debate about exactly who first domesticated dogs and when, it's largely agreed on that the practice began nearly fifteen thousand years ago, initiated by hunter-gatherers.

How do we know they were hunter-gatherers? Because that's the only kind of human society that existed until our long-lost ancestors enlisted wolves to work beside them. Dogs were the first of all domesticated animals, and without them all the domestications that followed—chickens, sheep, goats, pigs, cows, horses—well, they might never have happened.

It's easy to sit back now and imagine an orphaned puppy wandering up to prehistoric man's fire one night and setting this all in motion, but it hardly seems like one isolated case could bring us to where we are today—with nearly ninety million dogs living as pets in the US alone.

A Metamorphosis

There are tons of theories about just how the domestication of wolves began—with scientists continuing to cull more information from ancient bones as DNA technology improves. Even with the wealth of data available, most theories come back to the idea that this didn't happen in a single place and then from there spread around the world. More likely, ancient humans and wolves found their way to one another in multiple locations across the globe at roughly the same time.

We may never know exactly how a wild creature became human's best friend, but one leading theory argues that in the beginning, wolves more or less domesticated themselves. Seeing opportunities to scavenge food and maybe gain security by getting near a fire, a few brave, nondominant wolves may have chosen to live near and even interact with humans. If their approach was friendly and deferential, it might have increased their odds of survival—meaning that survival of the fittest and survival of the friendliest might have been one and the same.

Considering how humans have treated wolves throughout history—hunting them to near extinction across most of the globe—a theory of wolves coming *to* us may hold more water than one of us trying to live cooperatively with them. As the animal we now call "dog" adapted and integrated into civilization, the wolf did not. In fact, as man evolved from hunter to herder with incalculable help from the domesticated dog, the wolf became a fierce competitor in the race for survival.

However it started, the partnership of these two intelligent, independent, family-oriented (pack-oriented) species changed the world for both of us. With each generation, the wolves who found their way into human communities became a little less feral and a little more tuned in to people. That adaptation alone—paying attention to our body language, gestures, and even facial expressions—was a game changer. It opened the door to training, working together, and fostering attachments between our species. After all, an animal that cares what you think, what you want, and whether you are physically present can be more easily trained than one that finds you either terrifying or beneath its notice.

Studies show that the dog breeds genetically closest to wolves are also the ones that are the least tuned in to human actions and voices. Even more interesting, evolutionary biology studies have found that many of our pet dogs' traits seem to have been selected—naturally or deliberately—to keep them in a state of arrested development compared with their wolf ancestors. This might help explain why dogs are often so amenable to being coddled and trained (things adult wolves absolutely won't tolerate), and it might even offer a little insight into some of the physical features that make adult dogs appear more like wolf puppies than like wolf adults. Characteristics like wide, round eyes and soft, floppy ears—those just don't exist among mature wolves.

The Wild Side

Over the years, I've had numerous opportunities to work with modern wolves. They're not the same creatures that roamed the earth fifteen thousand years ago, but they're the closest thing to them that exists today. Trying to get cooperation from a wolf is actually more like trying to train a bear or a cheetah than it is like working a dog. They don't listen, don't look at you, and don't give a damn about what you want them to do. Instead, they avoid contact as much as possible, pace incessantly, and bolt at the slightest provocation. They're large, independent, wired and wary bundles of energy that deserve to be treated with respect and given a wide berth.

For this reason, I often work with hybrids when a job demands a wolf-looking animal be trained for television or movies. These dog-wolf hybrids look the part, but their mixed genetic makeup means that they're capable of learning basic commands—and that I can usually get them to work without them going completely rogue.

I start my training with new dog owners by explaining the five common characteristics of dog-wolf hybrids. Why? Because they offer a unique glimpse into the genetics of dogs *and* wolves—both how they are the same and how they differ. All encapsulated within a single animal. They also allow new clients the opportunity to understand how the wolf instincts in their dog might be magnified, helping them more easily identify mannerisms and behaviors that are wolflike. It's amazing how often the wolf side of a hybrid—even if the animal's bloodlines are primarily from dogs—bubbles up and distinguishes these animals from everyday dogs.

I've also (as you can probably imagine) had countless calls from *owners* of these hybrid wolf-dogs looking for help with training problems, and examining these problems can help us understand just how important a role wolf genetics plays in dog behavior. These are extreme cases because of the animals' unique breeding, but they drive home the point that even a little bit of wolf DNA goes a long way. Even when a hybrid is genetically *mostly* dog, the key issues that crop up in a family-pet scenario offer a spot-on list of the wolf characteristics we see in our pet dogs.

Throughout the book, I'll talk about how these traits (and others that are part of your dog's genetic makeup) influence day-to-day behavior, but let's start with five of the species-defining wolf traits and just how much of an issue they can be when they show up in your pet dog.

One caution: people often romanticize wolves as the ultimate independent, powerful, graceful animal. It's hard to argue with that. But sometimes wolf enthusiasts end up going so far as to adopt these dog-wolf hybrids as pets. Hybrid buyers tend to think they're bringing home tame wolves, creatures that look wild but behave like shepherds or huskies. In reality, a hybrid is a genetic roll of the dice—and you're not likely to truly know what you're dealing with until the animal reaches maturity. At that point, these dogs often end up being much more wolf than almost any household can handle, and in the end both the animals and the families end up unhappy. These outcomes, in addition to the legal entanglements that can arise from owning a hybrid, are enough to make me recommend against buying them as pets. Besides, right this minute there are millions of dogs of every known breed and breed combination sitting in shelters, running out the odds and the clock on finding forever homes. Why not welcome one of those dogs into your life instead of trying to force a relationship with a dog-wolf hybrid that may never truly be comfortable being part of your pack?

While every individual animal is different, this is especially the case with hybrids. Some of these wolf-dogs are manageable pets that get along with other dogs and with their families. But some are incredibly difficult—even impossible—to live with. Unfortunately, there's no way to predict which way one animal might go because there's not even a hint of a breed standard for them, and deliberately mixing the genes of two completely different species is tricky business. This kind of genetic outcross does not work in exact mathematical percentages (i.e., 50 percent wolf). Even if it did, having one wolf parent and one dog parent doesn't mean the resulting pup's genes will be divided equally. Instead, most hybrids are the genetic equivalent of pulling the handle on a slot machine loaded with all possible genetic outcomes. There's no way to predict which characteristics will come up.

5 Common Wolf Traits

1. Shyness. If you take Hollywood's word for it, wolves are bold, aggressive creatures that dominate everything in their orbit. Sounds great, but that image is pure fiction. With few exceptions (read on to meet Theo, who is one of them), wolves are among the shyest creatures on the planet. They prefer to be invisible, and they go to great lengths to avoid interaction unless they're breeding or hunting. In the wild, keeping to the shadows is a first-rate survival tool. But in your home, it can be a disaster.

A decade ago I got a call from a young couple who had adopted a hybrid puppy, Rex. They were hoping to have a dog with just enough wolf DNA to look and act a little wild. For the first months, the relationship was everything they'd wanted, but like most canines, Rex started showing his true personality as he got close to a year old and began to mature. Day by day, the puppy was fading, and in its place a creature with a big problem was emerging. Rex was terrified—of bicycles, passing cars, other dogs, strangers, and even the *sidewalk*. The hybrid wasn't just a little worried about these things; he went full duck-and-cover every time he encountered any of them. Since the owners lived in a city apartment, Rex's phobias meant that each trip to take him out to relieve himself or get any exercise quickly became a stressful, frustrating, and sometimes frightening situation.

By the time they called me, the couple who had dreamed of

raising a near-wolf were dreading every time they had to take Rex outside. All three of them were miserable.

I wish I could say that I was able to modify this animal's behavior so he could stay in his home. I've spent years of my life doing just that for *dogs* with extreme fears, bad habits, and obedience issues. But *wolves* don't do obedience, and there are times when nature simply overpowers nurture. This was one of them. Rex's innate fear of the unfamiliar wasn't just part of how he behaved: it was a cornerstone of his being. No matter how often, how gently, or how consistently Rex faced the city streets with his owners by his side, his panic didn't subside. The inner wolf, the genetic part of this hybrid that was supposedly his recessive side, was front and center, and his personality was not budging.

Shyness is considered an aberrational behavior in any dog, and people have spent thousands of years deliberately and carefully breeding it out. Despite that, it happens anyway, sometimes because of those wolf genetics creeping in, and sometimes because of environmental factors—things that happen to a dog during its life. Some dogs become shy as a result of abuse, but the most common cause is plain old poor socialization. A common example is a puppy raised in a kennel with little human contact or interaction with the world. An extreme example is an Australian cattle dog I recently rescued who had lived her entire life in a single, filthy, unprotected outdoor kennel in a breeding facility. This is a dog who had never worn a collar or been for a walk on a leash, who had never had any opportunity to bond with a person, who was panicked at the sound of human voices and the sight of us working with the animals around her. This was a dog who literally dug down into the ground and hid in a hole rather than be touched by a human hand. Yes, she was shy, but that was completely out of character with her breed. ACDs are typically confident and outgoing and pretty darn fearless.

There are no breeds that have been deliberately developed to be shy, but the trait still sometimes seeps into individual animals, part of their legacy from their wolf forebears. The one group I see this in most often is white shepherds, but even then it's not every dog. A wider group that can be prone to shyness is small dogs. This likely boils down to the simplest self-preservation logic: if you're a five-pound animal living in a world of giants, you're smart to be a little timid to help ensure that you don't get hurt.

Whether a dog's shyness is caused by environmental factors or genetics, there's a good chance it can be eased with patience, time, and training.

2. A Need for Space. Another trait wolves and hybrids feel deeply is their drive to roam. In the wild, a typical wolf pack commands a territory of at least fifty square miles, sometimes much more. The pack hunts this land, covering it efficiently on foot, and it's not uncommon for a wolf to rove twenty to thirty miles in a single day. In fact, the thing I remember most vividly about the wolves in my uncle's menagerie is that in order to keep them content, they needed more space than nearly any other animal we worked. The lone wolf's enclosure was nearly the size of a football field—and even with all that space he was constantly, endlessly checking and testing the perimeter.

You can pick a fifty-mile area in any city in the US right now and find thousands of dogs who are perfectly happy to share that space with one another as long as they've got a couch or a corner or a crate to call their own, but it doesn't work that way for wolves.

For Rex, the need for extreme levels of territory and exercise compounded the problems that arose from his fear of the sights and sounds of the city. This was an animal who was never going to be content (or in his extreme case, even healthy) living in an apartment and getting outside a handful of times a day. Rex needed room to run, and eventually he got it. I put his owners in touch with a Northern California rancher with hundreds of acres of land and extensive experience dealing with hybrids. Rex's first family made the hard choice—the right choice—in acknowledging that they couldn't give him the kind of home he needed. Rex went on to live an independent, rural life on the ranch, and the couple was able to channel all the energy and affection they had for a pet into a 100 percent dog who quickly adapted to their lifestyle and home.

The wolf's drive to cover and command a wide territory boils down to ensuring that it has enough resources to survive, and the hybrid still felt those same urges. The idea that a modern dog breed requires "room to roam," however, is largely a fallacy. What we do have are many dogs (especially those with roots in the herding, hound, and working groups) with extremely high exercise needs. Those needs may be more easily met if you've got a big fenced yard, but they can also be satisfied with daily runs, hikes, or trips to the dog park. The higher your dog's energy and prey drive, the more exercise they'll likely need (and the more determined they'll be to get it). On the other hand, most of the true "roamers" I encounter these days are unneutered males (and females in heat). If your dog falls into this category, please consider having them neutered or spayed. As someone who encounters thousands of unwanted dogs every single year in shelters and on the streets, I promise you that this simple act is a service to the species.

3. Territoriality. Yet another family that called me with wolf-dog troubles reached out when their pet seemed to suddenly outgrow her house-training. It had initially worked, so they were certain she was capable of managing her bodily functions, but as she approached eighteen months old, the hybrid began not only marking (peeing) throughout the house but also getting testy around the bed and food dish.

The territoriality of a wolf is intense, and it's not an easy problem to deal with. Wolves in their natural environment are in constant competition for mates, land, and food. The moment they're old enough to exert dominance over resources, they do so. When you try to fight that, you are pushing back on tens of thousands of years of evolution spurring these animals to protect what's theirs.

Today's dogs are a long way removed from these urges, but we still see them sneak into modern canine behavior. The most obvious (and probably the most offensive) form is urine marking by unneutered males. The best solution is prevention—neutering the dog before marking becomes a habit. Resource guarding is a more common problem, one that I see all the time and can almost always help owners come up with strategies and training steps to fix. This can happen with any dog breed, but it's most common among those bred to be strong-willed and independent workers. Dogs from the working and herding groups are the most likely to need a little help in this area. It's worth noting that any dog can develop resource-guarding behaviors if it's actually struggling to get by. In my work rescuing strays who have been abandoned in both urban and rural areas, I encounter dogs who are competing with other dogs just to survive. In those conditions, almost any dog can rightfully start to behave more like a wolf and less like a pet.

4. Fierce Independence. This can take a lot of forms, but there are a couple that anyone dreaming of owning a wolf or wolf-dog should know. The first is that, in contrast with domesticated dogs, wolves don't bond with people. Like most wild species, they stick with their own. There's no way to measure (or underestimate) the difference this makes in the relationship between people and wolves versus people and dogs. Most pet dogs feel an almost gravitational pull toward their people; it's one of their defining characteristics. That closeness is the foundation for the connections we build—walking, playing, training, even napping together.

Second, wolves don't rely on people to feed them. While dogs, even untamed ones, are largely scavengers, wolves are primarily carnivores who hunt their own food. This fact takes on new meaning when you try to train an animal that is not motivated to work for food rewards. Even if I am able to get a wolf's attention and engage it, if I try to train with treats, I'm likely to be ignored. Given the options and its genetic drive to hunt self-sufficiently, a wolf is more likely to decide to forget me and find its own food than it is to learn to sit, stay, or roll over for it.

Years ago I got an up-close-and-personal taste of this while working with a hybrid on a movie set. This dominant female lived with a pack of other hybrids. They were not well socialized to people, and they were definitely not what you or I would consider trained. When I walked into their enclosure, several of them rushed me, jumping up, poking my face with their muzzles. It wasn't an attack; it was an inspection. I put my hand up, calmly but firmly blocking them and gently but persistently pushing them away. The trick in this kind of situation is to project neutrality, so I wasn't friendly, I wasn't scared, and I definitely wasn't aggressive. The female I was working that day was named Freya, and she had an intense, intimidating manner and no interest whatsoever in working with a trainer. I needed her to bare her teeth, and it quickly became clear it wasn't going to happen by teaching her to smile. Instead, we ended up holding her in a harness on one side of the set and suspending one of her favorite bones from a boom across the way. When we poked the bone with a stick, the cameraman got footage of all the teeth he could handle. Freya may not have been open to traditional training, but she knew her bone when she saw it! This is a perfect example of working with natural wolf behavior in a very wolfy hybrid.

5. Prey Drive. Any animal—even a domesticated one—can exhibit defensive aggression when it feels threatened. Prey-driven aggression is something else—and it's strongest in carnivores who need to survive on what they can catch. Wolves fall squarely into this category. Pet dogs carry the remnants of this drive, but they typically exhibit it in less lethal ways. In the next chapter we'll look at some of the ways selective breeding has harnessed dogs' prey drive and taken the bite out of it (pun intended). First, though, let's talk about what a disaster that functional drive can be if it falls to a person to try to manage it.

My friend Kevin is a big guy and a good dog owner. A few years ago he brought home a hybrid and named him Theo. For the first year things went pretty well. As the dog matured, though, his inner wolf started coming out in increasingly intimidating ways—both in terms of his appearance and in his actions. Initially, he became destructive in the house, tearing up furniture and chewing through doorframes for no apparent reason except maybe boredom. Outside, things were worse. The dog could leap the six-foot fence around the property with almost no effort, and once he was on the other side, he began developing a serious case of dog aggression.

Even though this was a well-fed, well-cared-for animal, in the yard or out in the neighborhood, Theo would spot a dog and his whole body would stiffen. His ears would pin back, and he'd lower his shoulders and inch ahead stealthily, completely focused on his "prey." Within seconds, he'd lunge, and when he got to the end of the leash, he'd pull with all his might. This behavior was prey drive, pure and simple. To put the situation in perspective, consider that Theo was a 120-pound dog-wolf hybrid, tall and lean, with bushy gray fur that thickened around his chest and shoulders like a mane. He had a prominent snout, piercing gold-tinged eyes, and longer, thicker canine teeth than you've ever seen on a straight-up dog. When Theo walked down the sidewalk, people would stop and stare. When he pulled his prey-chasing routine, they'd run inside and bolt the doors.

Lots of dog breeds look intimidating, but this was different. As he matured, everything about Theo declared not only that he was descended from wolves but that in a different life he would have been destined to be an alpha predator.

Needless to say, being responsible for Theo's behavior was a huge task for Kevin. By the time I got involved, the situation had gone far past inconvenient and into dangerous.

In this case, with a strong owner who was willing to put the time and energy into training (and who was the sole adult in a household with no children to consider), we were able to modify Theo's behavior enough for Kevin to keep him. Kevin did so with the understanding, though, that his hybrid would require close supervision and regular conditioning every day for the rest of his life.

Prey drive is a common concern of dog owners, and perhaps your dog has shown signs of a strong prey drive (crouching, lunging, chasing, and maybe even mouthing or biting). Keep in mind that your dog descended from a highly prey-driven animal that relied on hunting and killing in order to survive. Prey drive is not something you can train out of your dog, but it is something you can absolutely control and lean into. Keep reading to find out more.

The Wolf Within

As different as wolves and modern dogs are, DNA does not just disappear, even after thousands of years. Traces—sometimes faint and sometimes robust—still live in breeds from the mighty Malinois to the small-but-scrappy Chihuahua. Some of the biggest points of friction between people and pets come down to these residual wolf genetics. Dogs who are off like a shot at the sight of a squirrel. Dogs who get growly around the food bowl. Dogs who insist on marking in the house. Dogs who lose their minds after a single day without exercise.

Knowing that these behaviors aren't because of anything you did or didn't do in training is the first step in learning to manage them. Second? Recognize that you're never going to completely wipe that wolf DNA away. Instead, in Part 2, we'll look at dozens of issues as they play out among different breed groups and establish tactics to curb or replace them with more acceptable options that'll make sense to your dog.

But first, let's take a look at how our own species' selective breeding choices going back thousands of years have shaped the breeds and functions of today's dogs.

A HISTORY OF DOGS
DOING JOBS

Knowing that our dogs come from wolves and how important the vestiges of that DNA are takes us part of the way to understanding their behavior. The next big piece of the puzzle comes from looking at the history of dogs at work.

I often get to train dogs for modern-day helping jobs—intelligent, dedicated service dogs who make life a little easier for people with physical limitations, and patient, gentle support dogs for those who live with emotional trauma. Sometimes I get to work with dogs for other, less conventional jobs, too. Dogs like Atticus, an Anatolian shepherd trained as a livestock guardian who ended up in a shelter because he was deemed too much of a lover and not enough of a protector. He learned to guide a teenaged girl with impaired vision—stopping at every change in grade so she knew she needed to step up or down. And Olive, an adorable, sweet-tempered poodle mix who learned patience and courtroom etiquette so that she could accompany, comfort, and empower kids while they testify in custody hearings. And Tank, the smart, loving Labrador retriever who learned not only to recognize when his diabetic owner's blood sugar dropped in the night but also to wake him so that he could correct it.

Each of these working dogs was once abandoned, destined to live or die in a shelter kennel—even though all of them possessed the potential to accomplish remarkable, finessed work.

So where did that potential come from? In essence, every job our dogs do today—from detecting bombs to fetching the paper to the deceptively easy-looking work of sitting silent and stoic on a child's lap in a courtroom—harks back thousands of years to the first work that domesticated dogs did side by side with people. In the beginning, jobs fell into one of two categories: hunting or guarding.

Over time, those tasks that dovetailed with dogs' natural instincts became specialized through a combination of natural selection and breeding—ultimately making the training of dogs like Atticus and Olive and Tank possible. Dogs like Atticus represent one of the earliest working-dog types to evolve—ancient flock guardians who stood sentinel over herds of sheep and goats. The work that Olive does represents another time-honored tradition—that of dogs bred to be doting and protective companions for the high and mighty, especially the ladies of European courts. And dogs like Tank represent centuries of purpose-focused specialized breeding to create animals who loyally hunt and retrieve on land and in the water.

All the while this evolution was taking place, something else was also happening—something that transcends any explanation that focuses solely on humans and dogs having a working relationship. A deep bond was forged between our species, one that's gone from strength to strength as the centuries roll past. These days it's easy to think of it as simply love, but the origins of this connection are more complex. Cooperation between people and dogs allowed both species to thrive. We've taken care of each other for so long and on so many levels that either would be lost without the other.

We Go WAY Back

To appreciate just how long this relationship has been evolving, you can look at almost any ancient civilization and find dogs with pride of place. Ancient Egyptian art doesn't just show dogs working, it shows them sitting at the bases of thrones, wearing collars and sporting leashes. When archaeologists found those collars deep in the Pyramids and translated their markings, they found names—names like *Reliable* and *Brave One*, and even a poor pup called *Useless*.

Across the Mediterranean Sea in ancient Greece, the archetype of man's best friend came to life in the form of Homer's Argus—the devoted hound who mourned and waited for his master while Odysseus spent ten years at war and another ten trying to get home. Both are old and tired when they meet again, and it is only Argus who recognizes the long-lost hero. The war-hardened man tears up at the sight of his loyal companion, and the dog can finally rest in peace after seeing his master's return. This is a dog who's on par with Lassie and Old Yeller—but his tale of love and loyalty precedes them by nearly three thousand years. Clearly, between the time of the wolves and the time of our oldest documented civilizations, the relationship between dogs and humans had deepened.

The faithful dog who waited for the grizzled veteran to come home from war inspired the name of the Argus Service Dog Foundation. Through it, co-founder Mike Herstik and I have the privilege of training skilled service dogs for disabled veterans. Our trainees are a testament to the intelligence, strength, affection, and devotion of man's best friend. I like to think that they're even worthy of being held up to the original Argus—the dog who represents the epitome of canine loyalty.

By the way, you'll encounter Mike from time to time in these pages. Besides being my partner in the foundation, he's a world-renowned detection dog trainer, and one of my most respected professional mentors.

Working Around the Globe

You won't find two wolves anywhere on the planet who look as different from each other as, say, a Doberman pinscher and a cocker spaniel. Humans had a strong hand in that, selectively breeding dogs for both physical and behavioral characteristics and creating the vast variety of breeds we have today. But long before the first breed standard was established, there were already differences in dogs based on a combination of natural adaptations and human influence that helped them survive and thrive in their unique environments. Tundra dwellers, for example, evolved to keep a layer of fat under their dense, double-coat fur. Desert dogs on the sunbaked African plains grew lean with sparse, short, light-colored coats. Over thousands of years, many regions fostered the evolution of landrace dogs—animals that share common traits thanks to both the guiding hand of evolution and deliberate selection based on purpose. Inevitably, form followed function, with dogs' bodies and minds shaped by the jobs they had to perform.

Everywhere humans migrated, dogs migrated, too, and as they spread region to region, the landraces morphed to suit their circumstances—getting taller or smaller, lighter or darker, more forceful or more docile. In some cases, like the saluki, the resulting dogs became cultural treasures and eventually formalized breeds.

Others weren't as fortunate, joining the millions of street dogs and pariah dogs who fend for themselves all over the world. When I went to Egypt, the streets were crowded with "baladi" dogs—town dogs that share a mix of features inherited from landrace sight hounds. In Cairo alone, millions of these animals live on the streets, in cautious proximity to humans, but not in the comfort and security of our homes.

Form Follows Function

Historians can pinpoint proof of ancient dogs hunting, herding, guarding, battling, and pulling sleds. In fact, there are cliff carvings on the Arabian Peninsula depicting leashed dogs accompanying hunters with bows and arrows that are estimated to be nearly ten thousand years old. Those pictures predate the invention of gunpowder, paper, formal systems of writing—even the wheel.

Without a doubt, the first jobs dogs did for humans were things they came by naturally—like using their superior sense of smell to locate prey, running that prey down at staggering speeds, and fiercely protecting their packs and territories from all comers. These were skills that, if they could be managed, would benefit a human family as much as a canine one.

We know ancient cultures did find ways to harness those abilities and to suit them to their purposes. For thousands of years, everywhere you found dogs, you'd find them doing meaningful work. Some were bred to enhance their abilities to sight prey, some to smell it, and some to run it down. Some were bred to maintain (and even accentuate) their instincts to kill prey, and others were bred to quash it. Some were bred to be cuddled and carried; others for baiting and biting. A noble tradition of herding dogs was born, leading to breeds that specialized in driving animals over long treks or bedding them down in the same place each night, watching over their safety or exacting compliance from them, working equally effectively with animals large and small, meek and mighty.

Generation after generation, the dogs became more specialized, and they took on increasingly complex and expanded roles in our lives. Neapolitan mastiffs fought in the Roman wars. Terriers chased and killed the mice and rats that were eventually determined to be the source of the bubonic plague. Bloodhounds tracked deer for hunters. Border collies commanded flocks and were promptly obeyed. Poodles dove into lakes and ponds to retrieve ducks and geese. Each of these breeds and dozens of others were fashioned over hundreds (sometimes thousands) of years, with their physical and behavioral traits constantly evolving to suit practical purposes.

And then the jobs went away.

With the exception of a tiny percentage, today's pet dogs don't work. We don't need them to fight, track, retrieve, intimidate, or kill anything. In fact, we prefer that they don't. Many are born with strong drives and the form to follow them, but no need. This simple fact is the root of much—if not most—of the problem behaviors I see as a trainer. Our ancestors spent the last several millennia devising a group of breeds, each of which could do a specific job like nobody's business, and now most of them are "just" dogs. They're our friends, our playmates, our roommates—but we don't need them to work.

Sometimes this is a great deal for the dogs, but sometimes it's a problem waiting to manifest.

In the coming chapters, we'll take a deep dive into each of the major dog groups (and we'll start with the biggest group of all—mixed breeds) to look at common ways that this manifestation takes place.

Practical or not, there is a purpose behind every unique characteristic.

When you look at your dog, no matter what breed, the vestiges of wolves are still there. The residue of the work its ancestors did is still there. The choices that breeders made over centuries to influence appearance and temperament and ability are still there. The purposes for those adaptations may have waned, but the traits are built to last.

People like to debate the influences of nature and nurture, but I think we all understand that both play a role. The thing is, your dog was born with a predetermined set of genetic components. Without acknowledging that side of the lifetime of behavior ahead, you're doing the nurture side of things in half measures. Understanding the nature piece of the equation gives you an edge in being the kind of effective, affectionate companion your dog needs.

The implications of knowing and understanding your dog's breed origins are significant. Your dog's instinctive drives help shape how she perceives the world and everything happening around her. If you can gain any insight into that perception, you can be a better trainer, a better playmate or partner, and a better owner. Years ago when I was working with a respected horse trainer, he told me, "The first thing you have to remember is that the horse is an animal of escape." This simple insight helped me adjust my body language, my tone, and my training techniques to better suit the animal in front of me. There are so many truths like this with dogs—so many instincts that have been developed (and then sometimes forgotten) that can help us understand where the animal is coming from, what makes it tick, what brings out its worst behavior, and what makes it feel fulfilled and happy.

As you read these chapters that detail my experiences with individual breeds and breed groups, know that these are my informed opinions, based on training thousands of dogs. There are always exceptions, and there are always people who are ready to either love or hate some dogs based solely on their history. My goal is to help you integrate that history into the way you manage your dog. Look at it this way. If you want to hear all the attributes of a car, go talk to a salesperson at a dealership. If you want to know the whole truth—the best features but also the places and conditions where things might break down or go wrong—ask a mechanic. I've spent the past decade working day in and day out with dogs from all kinds of backgrounds, doing inspections, tune-ups, and even total training overhauls. It's that immersion in behavior that has made me realize more with every passing year that the best way to own, exercise, bond, and train any dog is to work with their instincts, not to spend your life pushing back against them.

PART TWO

THE STORY OF YOUR DOG

Each chapter in Part 2 features an in-depth look at a specific dog group, and the breeds and behaviors that define that group. I start each chapter with the story of a dog in my own life. I want to highlight them here as a reminder that it's impossible to separate the story of your dog from the story of the two of you together. My knowing and understanding of each of my dogs helps make us a pack.

To find out what breeds are present in your dog, I recommend using the genetic testing information in Appendix B. Regardless of breed, I encourage you to read through all the information in this book. Chances are you'll find some common behaviors from each breed group that will help you better understand not only your dog but also the dogs of friends and family members.

THE LUCKIEST DOGS
ON THE BLOCK:
MUTTS AND MIXED BREEDS

I once trained a corgi–cane corso mix named Polo over several weeks. This dog had a thick, long body, giant shoulders, and a wide, square head—all of it perched on stocky four-inch legs. He lumbered when he walked, but when he got running, he could turn on the speed. Strangers would stop and do a double take at this guy, trying to figure out what the heck they were seeing. But you know what? The dog was as sweet as could be. He was smart and eager to learn. He was protective but not aggressive. He mastered his 7 Common Commands in a matter of a few days, and he was quickly conditioned to do them on automatic. When he graduated out of my care, I wished him a happy, healthy life with his family. I knew I'd always remember him fondly because he was such an unusual dog, but I didn't think I'd be seeing him again.

A year later I got a call from Polo's owners saying something had changed. They were worried. Their easygoing but powerfully built dog had suddenly started acting very protective of the wife. Nothing had changed in the household, but Polo was worried and on high alert.

I headed out to their place to see my old corgi–cane corso friend. He greeted me with a big grin, running my way at full steam, butting my leg with his head, then wriggling around and waiting to be petted. (Don't let anybody tell you dogs don't remember who their friends are, because they definitely do.) When I went in the house and followed the owner to the kitchen, though, Polo's demeanor changed. He sat down between me and her, and he basically body blocked me from getting within six or eight feet of her for the remainder of that visit. Worse, the husband said he'd been getting the same treatment—even an occasional growl.

We talked about their schedule, Polo's exercise, anything that might be causing this problem, but nothing jumped out as an explanation. In the end, we agreed an obedience refresher course would help get the dog back on track. Before his first session, though, Polo's owners got the big news that the wife was pregnant. *Aha.* Seems the dog was the first to know. I've seen this protective instinct kick in so many times—it's just one of the mysteries of how our species look out for each other. As the pregnancy progressed, Polo continued to be protective but was never aggressive. In addition, he started gently but insistently herding the mom-to-be, trying to keep her safe and insulated from the wider world. The couple worried that the dog might be hostile to the baby because of this, and all I could tell them was that in my experience I have yet to meet a dog that's protective of the mom and not of the infant.

When the time came, I helped them proceed with caution, making sure Polo had plenty of opportunities to see and smell the new baby from a safe distance, and then slowly increasing his access. Turns out this big, goofy, awkwardly shaped, energetic, and protective dog was gentle as a lamb with the new addition.

Polo was playful like a corgi—and a little bossy like one, too. He was loyal and protective like his cane corso forebears. He was loving and sweet, grateful for his home, and devoted to his people like a dog who's been rescued and given a forever family. He was basically a one-foot-tall and three-foot-long living, breathing example of everything I love about mutts.

About three quarters of the dogs in the world are mixed breeds. Their numbers include everything from dogs who are born to the streets and spend their lives there, to countless mixed-breed dogs who find their way to comfortable and loving forever homes, to costly "hybrid" pups, aka "designer breeds." I want to start the breed-specific chapters here because, as mentioned, most dogs fall into this category. If yours is one of them, I hope that after reading about mixed breeds and mutts, you'll dive into each of the next chapters to figure out what might be motivating your unique dog.

This chapter is broken down into two subsets: the deliberately blended designer breeds that have become wildly popular over the past twenty years, and the mutts of nearly every possible breed combination that naturally result from dogs being dogs. Historically, these mixes were the foundation of landraces around the world—regionally similar dogs adapted to the weather, terrain, and resources of a particular place. Today, with widely varied breeds living in proximity to each other all over the world, anything can happen, including some extremely strange pairings that result in dogs like Polo.

Working with mixed breeds, rescuing them and finding them homes, is a huge part of my life. Yes, there are purebred dogs who need homes, but thanks to breed-specific rescue networks, many of them are able to bide their time with foster families. Roughly 75 percent of dogs in shelters are mixed breeds, and among homeless dogs on the streets the percentage without a pedigree is likely even higher. As a result, most of the time when I'm training, I'm working with a dog that's got "mix" in its description. Sometimes I know a little about a dog's roots, like maybe that it's a boxer mix, poodle mix, or Lab mix. Sometimes it's hard to pin down a single breed, but easy to see that one group, like the hounds or the terriers, is heavily represented. Dogs have their tells, just like people, and when you see one circling up all the other dogs in the yard, pointing at every squirrel, or putting its nose to the ground and taking off at a run without so much as looking up, you're getting clued in to its genetic origins (in this case, one herding, one sporting, and one hound). Sometimes a dog is a genetic mystery at first glance—but then its hardwired traits bubble to the surface during play and training.

Even when the word doesn't come up, there's a good chance a dog is a mix. My dog Lulu, whom you'll learn about in Chapter 9, had paperwork from the shelter that deemed her a Chihuahua. It's not hard to see why—she was the right size, shape, and temperament to fit the bill. But then again, nearly every small dog that shelters can't put a breed on gets labeled Chihuahua. After years of wondering about Lulu's uniquely stubborn, feisty, sometimes aggressive and sometimes devoted personality, I sent a saliva sample away for a DNA test. The verdict explained a lot: my Chihuahua has less than 50 percent Chihuahua DNA. The balance of her genetics can be traced back to Pomeranians, Russell-type terriers, Pekingese, and yes, the most stubborn of breeds, the bulldog.

Doodles and More: Designer Mixed Breeds

Before we delve into the importance of breed for the Lulus and other mixes of the dog world, let's take a look at designer dogs. You know them by cutesy names like cockapoo, Labradoodle, golden doodle, puggle, and maltipoo. They are a rapidly growing "family" of dogs, one that's so in demand I'm seeing more of them with every passing week. Among those dogs, I see some shining examples of what can happen when everything in a genetic combination goes right, and less stellar examples of how it can all go wrong—so let's take a look at both.

Much of the designer breed craze started from a simple and legitimate need—people with allergies wanted pets (and wanted their family members to be able to have them). One of the first well-known dogs in this group was a Labradoodle named Sultan, bred for the specific purpose of providing a guide dog to a visually impaired woman who happened to have a spouse with allergies. Poodles are somewhat hypoallergenic (their hair doesn't shed to the extent of most dogs), and when you breed them with other dogs, their hair is typically dominant, creating hypoallergenic blends. Sultan, half Labrador retriever, half poodle, was a perfect solution for his owner, helping her achieve greater independence for a decade before his retirement.

So began what I sometimes call the *Let's get a poodle over here!* phase of dog breeding, as dozens of breeds were mixed with poodles of all sizes to create new dogs.

The breeder responsible for Sultan has gone on record saying he regrets releasing the "Frankenstein's monster" that is the Labradoodle, but I think he just sped up an inevitable process. People have been mixing dog breeds for centuries to achieve specific physical and behavioral traits. The process of fine-tuning dogs to be great workers and companions has always been and continues to evolve. So it was only a matter of time before mixes that nail today's most desirable traits—being calm, affectionate, predictable house pets—started cropping up and becoming just as popular and in demand as any purebred dog. Some of these "hybrids" and "blends" (call them "mutts" and you're likely to get an earful from their owners) are fads that quickly rise to and fall out of favor. Some endure and may eventually become recognized breeds in their own right. No matter what, they are helping shape the future of dog ownership.

Unfortunately, there's been an unexpected dark side to the doodle craze, because it has sparked a mind shift in the rescue world. Since the idea of hypoallergenic dogs started gaining attention, it seems like everybody wants one. Nearly every person who reaches out to me to find a shelter dog is requesting a hypoallergenic dog now. It's creating an impossible environment at shelters for great dogs who are being overlooked because they shed. If there are one hundred dogs at a shelter, odds are fewer than ten of them are hypo. Breaking news, folks: dogs shed.

Unless you're one of the small percentage with severe allergies, please get over it.

———

In my experience, there are some truly winning combinations among the designer mixes (including the Labradoodle and the golden doodle), but anytime there's wild demand for a dog, some less healthy and less stable examples are inevitable. The problem isn't the genetic combination of the two breeds—it's the way some unscrupulous people take advantage of demand for those puppies with *oodle* and *poo* in their names.

Blending breeds alters more than dogs' coats; it can also skew their personalities. For example, Mike Herstik solely used Malinois dogs for bomb-location work in the past. The problem that arose was that the Mal, aside from being an incredible working breed, is sometimes prone to being less than social, a bit intractable, and even destructive. Their drive and intensity can redirect in less than desirable behaviors when they're not working. Rather than accept this, Mike started using Malinois crossed with eastern European–type working German shepherds—a breed with quiet confidence and more tolerance for people. The shift worked, creating dogs with the athletic ability and focus of Malinois along with the biddable temperament of working line German shepherds. I've personally met and worked with Mike's Mal-shepherd blends, and their temperaments are like night and day compared with the purebred Malinois. These dogs are often referred to as "German Malinois," and they've become a favored working mix for both law enforcement and military teams.

Buyer Beware

If it sounds like these sometimes creative breed combinations might be too good to be true, that's because some of them are. One thing that's critical to remember about designer breeds is that they're harder to predict than any breed alone. Instead of taking one set of genes and getting whatever combination of that pool destiny serves up in your dog, you're getting some combination of two. People often mistakenly assume that they'll get the best of both breeds. It's possible, but it's equally possible you get the collection of genes you were hoping to avoid. For example, someone dreaming of a puggle might imagine a mash-up of the quiet playfulness of a pug with the sturdy health and athleticism of a beagle. That could definitely happen. What else could happen? You could get a dog with all the barking and howling of a beagle along with the respiratory and orthopedic problems that are common in pugs. There's just no logical way to do the math when breeding these dogs. It's canine gambling.

The most basic explanation is this: each dog has both genotype and phenotype. Genotype is the entire collection of a creature's genetic material. Think of it as a menu of everything that's possible. Phenotype, on the other hand, is a creature's observable physical traits. These are the genetic features that come to pass, thanks to some combination of what Mother Nature provided and environmental influence.

So the genotype for the puggle we're talking about contains a wide range of possibilities from each parent. This is an oversimplification, but if puggle genetics were a slot machine, you'd have symbols for things like a short nose or a long nose, a barky dog or a quiet dog, a high-energy dog or a moderate energy dog, a dog that might develop hip dysplasia and one not prone to it. Just among those few characteristics, when you pull the lever on that slot machine, there are scores of possible outcomes. Throw in thousands of potential genes, and you've got infinite possibilities.

The upshot of this is that anyone who owns or is thinking of owning a designer mix needs to know that dog breeding is nothing like making a Build-A-Bear. Even though some breeders would have you believe it's that simple, genetics are not entirely consistent or predictable. When you factor in that there's no oversight for these dogs, there are a lot of ways you can be taken advantage of when getting a designer pup. They can be wonderful dogs, and you can look at the histories of both breeds as you get a handle on their behavior and train them, but buyer beware: despite the extremely high prices some of these dogs command, you can't be certain of the outcome until your dog reaches maturity.

The Mutts We Love

As far as I'm concerned, the best thing about the designer breed craze is the subtext I'm seeing people pick up in different ways—the idea that mixed breeds are desirable dogs. I'm part of the brotherhood of dog owners who's known this about mixes in general and mutts in particular for a long time. After more than a decade of rescuing up to a hundred dogs each year—most of them mutts—then training them and finding them homes, I may be their biggest fan. I definitely owe them much of my career. One after another they've come into my life and proved the point that a shelter dog of unknown origin can make just as suitable, loving, and well-trained a pet as any other dog. Plus, the only way my single biggest professional objective—that of dramatically shrinking the number of dogs who end up in shelters in the first place—comes together is if mutts keep proving me right.

Mutt is a term I use with nothing but affection and respect, and I'm starting with this group because they truly are reflections of the genetic destiny of all dogs. Dogs for whom the alchemy of breed is something that just happens rather than something that's planned are the most common dog type in the world. Left to their own devices and on the streets, dogs aren't looking to keep a recognized breed's bloodline pure. Any breed will mate with any other—it's kind of the code of strays. From a health standpoint, mutts are sometimes the healthiest dogs, because the constant mixing of new genetics means fewer hereditary health problems like the breathing issues common in pugs or the heart conditions of Great Danes. Many of the health problems that have been created or exacerbated by breeding dogs for a certain look or a single behavior trait without enough regard for the traits that might come along for the ride are much rarer in mutts from diverse gene pools.

Mixed breeds also live longer, on average, than purebred dogs.

From a behavior standpoint, though, a true mutt can keep you guessing until their adult temperament reveals itself. In purebreds, what we know is based on common traits averaged out over millions of dogs. We have hundreds, if not thousands, of years of data for some breeds, so we know their typical traits. This is the one place where you can expect to see some stereotypes bear out. Nine times out of ten, herding breeds are high energy; terriers have heavy prey drive; and hounds are constantly searching for scent. If you have a breed type that doesn't fit the typical personality traits, they're the exception, not the rule.

When you're dealing with a mixed-breed dog, trying to figure out how to be the best handler and trainer is a unique challenge. This is where you become a better behaviorist. You have to spot the traits and behaviors that most define your dog. This is what trainers do when we assess dogs we don't know. We use any basic data we have about a breed type, and we identify other traits until we can form a game plan to resolve an issue or offer effective training. The guesswork isn't necessarily a bad thing, because doing it will make you more observant of your dog's behavior, her likes, dislikes, and quirks.

With that in mind, there are several steps you can take to make training and behavior modification easier on you and your mixed-breed dog.

Know Your Breed History

Even though most of the dogs I work with are mixed breeds, if I could start my dog-training career over again right now, the one thing I'd do differently is spend more time learning about breed histories and instincts. This is invaluable information in helping me know when to push a dog in training, when to ease off, and when to try a different tactic altogether. It helps me understand what is possible for a dog, and when I need to say *No* to a client who wants me to turn off a thousand-year-old instinct in a few thirty-minute sessions. Knowing a breed's history is vital to the training process. The pressure a Malinois can take when training versus the pressure a poodle can take is light-years apart. Knowing a breed's origins gives me the game plan I need to train them.

You've already started down this path of learning breed history by owning and reading this book, so pay close attention to the next few chapters if you're trying to match behaviors of your mutt with a particular breed.

Doggie DNA Testing

The science of evaluating dogs' DNA has improved leaps and bounds over the past several years. Companies started with baseline information for breed identification, but after testing tens of thousands of kits, they've been able to expand their databases and knowledge, and increase the accuracy of their results. Testing is the one shortcut to learning your dog's genetic makeup. The benefits go beyond satisfying your curiosity about Rover's parentage. Knowledge is power, and in this case it gives you insight into any likely medical issues your dog might develop as well as clues about its temperament and likely strengths and weaknesses in training. In recent years I've made it nearly mandatory that my clients do DNA tests on their mystery mutts. This gives me a game plan so that I can already have questions answered and save everyone a lot of training time. And when it comes to dog trainers, time is definitely money.

Look for Clues

Even without a DNA test, there are ways to "read" your dog's behavior and figure out how to customize training, play, and exercise options that work best for both of you. When I work a new dog, I'm watching to see certain things that'll guide my approach.

- What motivates the dog? Some dogs are snack hounds; some love to play; some won't tune in to you until it suits them.
- What does fun look like? Does your dog like chew toys? Fetch toys? Does he like to chase squirrels? Or roam the park pointing at birds? Is he drawn to the water, or to the joy of running full-out, or to playing with other dogs? Pay attention to the things that bring your dog joy because that's where you'll find your best training tools.
- How does the dog learn best? Just like kids, dogs have their own learning styles. Some require short bursts of training and plenty of rewards. Some love to work and will stick to it because it feels like a game to them. Some learn best in groups and others learn best alone. Knowing something about your dog's breed can help

determine your best approach, but this is also information you can glean from close observation.

Respect Instinct

Things go better for everyone involved if you respect your dog's instincts. That doesn't mean letting them run wild, but it does mean working within the framework of how they think and what they need. Having that context means that when you're having a hard time holding your hound's attention, you don't get mad: you get creative. It means you don't bother trying to restrain the energy in a pent-up herding dog. Give her the opportunity to burn off plenty of the day's energy. It means you give your terrier a place to dig instead of trying, futilely, to forbid digging altogether.

This especially means that when you're training or coping with behavior issues, take note if your dog keeps running into the same brick wall. If one method of problem-solving isn't working, try another. I had an Aussie shepherd at the ranch who set about herding my pack first thing in the morning and kept at it all day. At a certain point, the other dogs had had enough, and even the Aussie wasn't having fun anymore. The owner asked if I could teach the dog a NO HERDING command (and I honestly responded that it would be about as easy to teach as a NO BREATHING command). Instead, I taught the dog a reliable DOWN, and I incorporated the classic herding command of "That'll do," which basically means *knock it off*. The outcome was exactly what was needed—done in a way the dog could accept and embrace.

Conclusion

When people ask me what's the perfect dog, I always respond that it's an underdog—a mutt with a mix of features and personality traits both predictable and surprising. It may take a little more time to figure out what motivates your mixed-breed dog, but the rewards in terms of a well-trained dog and a loving companion are worth it. Mutts have given me so much. They've given me a career that I absolutely love. They gave me a hit network television series. They gave me the opportunity to travel the world and give keynote talks to large crowds about shelter dogs. Mutts have given me everything I have today . . . and for that I give back by educating them to the best of my ability, making sure they're as healthy as possible while they're with me, and finding them their forever homes. My knuckles have always bled for mutts. They gave me life. I'm always just repaying the favor.

HIGHLY SPECIALIZED MACHINES: THE WORKING GROUP

As a rule, I try not to ascribe too many human traits to dogs because it's so important to our relationship with them to respect the fact that they're not just furry people. Every once in a while, though, I meet a dog I think must have been meant to be human and just ended up in the wrong body. That was the case for my rottweiler, Remi. He was like a wise old man in a heavily muscled dog suit. Like most rotties, Remi was highly intelligent and easy to train. His breed's long-held job of being a guardian hasn't changed a whole lot in centuries—protect the herd, protect the estate, protect the apartment, protect the family. His instincts were everything you want to see in a powerful dog: watchful and judicious; never hair-trigger.

Rottweilers are also fiercely loyal, like take-a-bullet loyal, to their people, and Remi was no exception. I'd be gone for ten minutes to get the mail, and he would all but collapse with relief when I walked back in the door. This is a favorite breed of mine for their generally sweet nature, quiet confidence, and attentive intelligence.

Even though Remi was the picture of controlled power, he still occasionally managed to set off people's alarm bells because of his can't-be-ignored presence. One of the worst instances happened when we were out for a ride in Los Angeles. Remi *loved* to ride shotgun, hanging his big head out the window, watching and smelling the city as we cruised. On this particular afternoon, though, we started to pull away from a red light and a bicyclist came booking up alongside us. The sudden appearance of the biker, the speed at which he was moving, the fact that he got closer to the car than any of the pedestrians or other cars did—I'm not sure which element of it piqued Remi's protective instincts, but it was just enough for him to square his giant head and give one big, bellowing *WOOF* at the guy.

It was, as always, the exact right amount of force for the situation—just a verbal warning that was meant to say something like, *Too close*, and to warn me of the potential threat Remi perceived. It would have been a nonevent—except for the fact that my dog's single bark startled the biker. Over the next seconds he went from focused and plowing forward to wide-eyed and wobbling to ass-over-teakettle on the curb. He jumped up quickly to shake a fist at us, and I was glad to see he wasn't hurt. Remi watched it all happen and then, seeing that we weren't in any danger, relaxed and turned his attention back to the joy of the ride.

Even when he was totally relaxed, a part of that dog was always working.

On January 31, 1925, a small, willful, and intensely loyal Siberian husky who had earned his way from an unwanted runt of the litter to lead dog on a world-renowned sledding team leaned into his harness and set out on what would be history's most epic mushing trip. His name was Togo, and over the next twenty-four hours he would guide his team over eighty-four miles of icy Alaskan tundra, frozen waterways, and craggy mountains. Through temperatures that bottomed out below minus fifty, sixty-mile-an-hour winds, blinding snow, and utter exhaustion, Togo ran, pacing his team in a profoundly dangerous environment. Behind him on the sled, forty-seven-year-old Leonhard Seppala pushed himself and his dogs to their limits because he knew the package they carried—a twenty-pound metal box filled with snugly wrapped vials of diphtheria antitoxin—was the only thing standing between the population of Nome and an outbreak so deadly it threatened to wipe out every last man, woman, and child in the region.

Nobody who was tuned in to the drama of this expedition was ignorant of the stakes. It had been less than seven years since the 1918 flu pandemic killed an estimated fifty million people worldwide and devastated native and rural populations across Alaska. The prospect of another deadly, contagious disease outbreak was flat-out terrifying. When Nome's only doctor telegraphed an SOS for antitoxin, the problem wasn't as much supply as it was logistics. There was no way to move the vials fast enough to prevent the spread from spinning out of control—no roads, no rail, no viable air or water options. The limitations left only the oldest form of long-haul transportation in the tundra: the dog sled.

That's how 20 mushers and roughly 150 dogs ended up gutting their way through the lifesaving 674-mile serum run, with the longest leg and the most brutal terrain falling to Seppala and twelve-year-old Togo. The dog was over-the-hill by mushing standards, but he was the only one Seppala trusted with his life and those of the rest of his dogs. Togo was rugged and brave and seemingly impervious to the cold—and he didn't know how to quit.

Togo's feat of endurance and determination earned him a place among the most storied dogs in history—but the actual fame went mostly to the dog who ran the last leg of the run, the one who crossed the finish line in Nome and had his picture taken. For weeks after, photos of that dog, Balto, were plastered across newspapers around the world.

I think it's kind of fitting that Togo stayed under the radar compared with the dog who got the glory—because that's the fate of even the most amazing working dogs throughout history, up to and including today. We don't know the names of the other 148 dogs from the 1925 Serum Run to Nome. We don't know the ones who raced across World War II battlefields bearing messages and supplies on their backs. We don't know the dogs who've plucked sailors from freezing waters or fought off home invaders, or the ones who show up with their handlers after natural (and manmade) disasters, ready to search for and rescue survivors from the rubble. This is a group with a rich history of unsung heroes, past and present.

Ancient Breed Meets Modern World

On a seemingly unrelated note, I have a client who's lost his husky, Lena, at least a dozen times, sometimes for a few hours, sometimes for days. He used to call every other week to tell me this dog was out, again. There was no tracing Lena's movements—no favorite place she'd visit or hide. Every time she took off, her owner rightfully worried it might be the last.

Luckily, Lena always found her way home, and each time I helped this client beef up the enclosure. First, we raised the fence. Then we put cement around the posts. Then we put the whole thing on an incline.

Every time, Lena raised her game. When she dragged a patio chair across the yard and used it to launch herself over the fence, we realized that if she was ever going to be able to safely spend time outdoors, we'd need to go full-zoo and put a roof over it. I'm betting there are great apes and big cats sitting in world zoos right now that have had less time and thought invested in their enclosures than Lena had in hers.

Somewhere along the way during this process, my client asked me what he thought was the obvious question: Can't you train her to stop running away?

The answer, if you think about it, is just as obvious: this dog breed was thousands of years in development by the Chukchi tribe of northeast Asia, with generation upon generation further honing a body type and skill set. Early huskies were part of the culture, and that culture's survival relied on their ability to do their job. For millennia, the people of this ancient society selected only the strongest, heartiest, most determined pulling dogs—dogs who ran for the love of it—for breeding. I could no sooner teach Lena to lose her desire to run than I could teach her to walk on two legs or speak Spanish, because that action (or lack of action) would run counter to everything her body and mind evolved to do. Like a shark that has to keep moving in the water to survive—an eons-old adaptation about which it has zero choice—Lena's genetic code dictates her intense desire to run. It isn't her fault there's no equivalent for the work a sled dog is born to do in the suburbs of Los Angeles. What I needed to help her owner understand was that installing an adequate fence wasn't going to be enough. Unless he was willing to provide the physical and mental stimulation his dog required, Lena—an otherwise sweet, smart dog—would continue to seek ways to satisfy those powerful, primitive urges on her own.

Of all the dog breeds out there, the husky is the one that most has half of its mind, body, and soul still in the wild.

A World of Working Dogs

Huskies are just one breed in the broad and diverse working group—a category that encompasses history's war dogs and modern-day rescue dogs, water dogs and mountain dogs, ancient flock guardians and equally ancient big-game hunters ("big" in this context includes potentially deadly and daunting prey like boars, lions, and bears). Many of these dogs evolved both by natural selection and by deliberate breeding to become so highly specialized they were literally born to their work, showing inclinations to guard, hunt, chase, swim, or race without even a shred of training.

At their best, these breeds are marvels of form and function— or at least they used to be. Today, many of their jobs are obsolete (and in some cases—like, say, bull-baiting—seriously undesirable), and no matter what they were bred to do, the vast majority of our modern dogs are "just" pets. They're companions, exercise partners, playmates, and sometimes gentle guardians. The gap between thousands of years of breeding to do one job and the modern insistence that they do another is the root of miscommunication, frustration, and behavior problems on both ends of the leash. If you don't give due respect to your dog's origins, it's all too easy to end up with a pet like Lena— who spent the first two years of her life making futile attempts to fulfill the genetic destiny of an Arctic sled dog on a sunny quarter acre in Southern California. This is a dog whose breed was responsible for helping a whole segment of human society survive and thrive by essentially giving them a powered vehicle. It hardly seems fair to ask her and every other dog like her to shut down all the hardwired urges she was born with and live a whole different kind of life. Instead, if we make the effort to understand these dogs and meet their needs, we can help most of them adapt to home life and live happily as part of our families.

Key Traits

The dogs in this group are far too widely varied to be summed up by a single list of behavior traits. Among them, though, a few subgroups have history and habits in common.

Flock Guardian Traits

A Unique Kind of Pack Loyalty

These earliest working dogs, breeds that include the Anatolian shepherd, Bernese mountain dog, Great Pyrenees, and komondor, did their jobs by integrating with the livestock and protecting them from predators. Ideally, a flock guardian looks at the herd under its care and sees them as its pack. If you're the owner of one of these breeds, don't be surprised to find that it develops a natural affinity for watching over your kids or your cats or the other dogs on the block. Thousands of years of breeding dogs to "adopt" sheep, goats, and other flocks as their own responsibility doesn't just evaporate when the job goes away. Fair warning—this devotion doesn't necessarily take on a warm, fuzzy form. Just like parents, among these dogs there are warm nurturing types, and there are also gruff, impatient, and bossy ones.

Lack of Prey Drive

Nothing spells doom for a flock guardian faster than having one of two things happen: either the dog abandons his post to chase a passing rabbit, squirrel, or other moving temptation; or (even worse) it goes after a member of the flock while perceiving it as prey. To protect against this, guardians were selected for centuries to have a fairly low prey drive. This is a great trait if you have a flock guardian as a pet—it makes them much more manageable on leash.

Judicious Use of Power

An effective flock guardian must be aggressive enough to intimidate or even fight an invading predator, but benevolent enough to be trusted with the flock. These dogs were bred to be big and fearless, to be aggressive toward predators, but otherwise even-tempered. That balanced temperament is one of their most defining characteristics, though some breeds, like the Anatolian shepherd, are more assertive, and others, like the Great Pyrenees, tend to be gentler.

Durability

Most dogs with flock guardian roots are sturdy and strong, tolerant of all kinds of weather (often preferring colder temperatures), and tough over a wide range of terrain. To do their jobs effectively, they can't be fussy or fearful.

Independence

By definition, a capable flock guardian is able to work without direct supervision. They are not actually bred to take direction, but to follow their inherent protective temperament.

Protection Dog Traits

Size and Strength

It's no coincidence that the dogs originally bred to protect people are an imposing lot. You don't bring a Yorkie to war or post a cocker spaniel at your gate. These dogs have a type, and that type is large and muscular, commanding a certain amount of respect on sight.

Many of history's most storied protection breeds, including the mastiff, the cane corso, and the rottweiler, can trace their lineage back to the Molossus dogs—developed in ancient Greece but equally the war dog of choice for the Romans. As the Holy Roman Empire spread, so did the reach of the dogs they bred for protection and combat.

The pasts of these dogs include many jobs beyond the scope of protection, with some of them also droving, hunting, sport fighting, and pulling carts.

Dignity

I'll admit I see even the most intimidating of protection breeds break character and act like goofballs once in a while. In general, though, the personalities of these dogs are reserved and intelligent. They're watchful, paying attention to both the action and the mood in a room. Many have had their temperaments altered through selective breeding to leave their origins behind and be better suited as family dogs.

Confidence

Protection plus fearfulness does not compute. To be good at their jobs, these dogs needed to be aware of their power and comfortable with it. You can expect them to be, at a minimum, comfortable in their own skin. A lot of them have some swagger with that.

Territoriality

Throughout history, accomplished war dogs and guard dogs have earned their keep by harboring no doubts about what belongs to them and what they're charged to defend. It's no wonder these dogs tend to need clear boundaries.

Dominance

Not every dog can be an alpha, but you'll find more of them playing the part in this group than in most. Even as these breeds have diversified and in some cases become much gentler versions of their former selves, most are still quick to step into a dominant role if they sense a leadership vacuum.

Pulling Dog Traits

Stamina

Archaeological records tell us that dogs have likely been pulling sleds in the Arctic for over nine thousand years. That's a heckuva long time to fine-tune breed strengths, and no trait is more necessary in a sled dog than stamina. These dogs are easily capable of covering dozens of miles a day. They do not adapt well (or at all, really) to sedentary lifestyles.

Not all pulling dogs are sled dogs. In Europe butchers favored large dogs over horses as cart pullers. Butchers always had a steady supply of meat products to feed their large dogs as part of their trade, and any breed large and strong enough to pull a heavily laden cart was recruited into service.

Wanderlust

Great sled dogs are eager, curious, and not afraid of new experiences and places. This trait runs a little counter to most mammals' (and most dogs') natural fear of the unknown, but it's a great asset for these animals that have to be willing to push ahead in unfamiliar terrain and inclement weather.

Strength and Durability

You can't always see a sled dog's musculature for all their heavy, insulating fur, so they may not immediately catch your eye and make you think "athlete" like a greyhound or a boxer might. But looks can be deceiving. Sled dogs have such powerfully muscled legs and backs that they can run all day pulling twice their weight—work most of their giant flock guardian cousins couldn't handle.

Escape Artists

My friend's escape-prone husky is no exception. These dogs can be super resourceful when they put their minds to getting out. Many of them are especially determined and effective diggers—a behavior that may carry over from countless generations of dogs who would dig below the snow line at the end of each day and nestle out of the wind until morning.

Hunger

Being a finicky sled dog is a formula for death in the tundra. Dogs bred to do this kind of work had to be able to fill up on whatever was available, whenever it was available, and they had to be able to work for hours or even days on it. As a result, they tend to be especially attentive to food and to eat like there's no tomorrow.

Fisherman's Dog Traits

Strength

The two most prominent fisherman's dog breeds, the giant Newfoundland and its smaller counterpart the Portuguese water dog, are both powerfully built, each of them structured so that strength carries over into water just as well as on land. They're heavily muscled in their backs and back legs, with wide webbed feet, large-capacity lungs, wide rudder-like tails, and serious jaw strength—the better to pull in fishing nets like they were bred to do.

Affection

If you were going to breed a dog to be your constant companion on a fishing boat, you'd likely make sure it was one with a warm, friendly temperament, too. These breeds are rarely aloof, aggressive, or even nippy, because none of those traits would be tolerable in close quarters. They're among the breeds most likely to be compared to teddy bears.

Drawn to the Water

Anybody who's had a water dog of any kind knows this trait. Maybe yours tries to swim in its water bowl, or rolls around in puddles to get wet, or finds near-transcendent joy when you turn on the backyard hose on a hot day. Being drawn to the water runs deep in these breeds' DNA.

Fearless

Among working fisherman's dogs, fear is a bit of a deadly sin. These are dogs who need to be game for adventure, open to meeting new people, tough in any environment, and willing to brave danger in whatever form it takes. Today this bring-it-on mentality still stands in most of these dogs. They're not easily intimidated by anything.

Protective

Different breeds and individual dogs display a wide range of protective instincts, from animals who would give your wallet to an intruder to those who body block for you when they see the mail carrier coming. And then there's the rare extreme of dogs who would leap into an icy, roiling sea to haul your drowning self to safety. Fisherman's dogs fall into this last category, and over the course of their histories and those of their forebears, these dogs have performed remarkable rescues in water and on land. The thing that's most remarkable about these feats isn't so much that the dogs accomplished them: it's that in countless documented cases, they did it without anyone asking them to. These are dogs that are tuned in to their owners, paying attention, and naturally willing and able to protect their safety.

Behavior Challenges and Possible Solutions

Here's the secret a lot of folks in the dog world would just as soon keep under wraps: almost inherently, great working dogs don't always make great pets. Dogs who are able to perform focused, demanding tasks for hours on end without interruption (and often with minimal supervision) simply aren't necessarily wired to be calm, loving, cooperative members of human families. They need stimulation and function to be content (and in some cases they need it to be sane). The good news is that most of today's dogs, regardless of breed, aren't actually working dogs. They may physically resemble them, and they may exhibit many of their behavioral traits, but they're many generations removed from being expected to work long, exhausting, completely focused hours each day to earn their keep. Through selective breeding for more easygoing temperaments and better abilities to get along in homes, they've been modified—some more successfully than others—to make great pets. However, if you own one of these dogs, you may face some typical working dog problems.

Energy Overflow

Despite the modifications that make some of history's toughest and most dedicated working dogs mellow enough (sometimes just barely) to move indoors and share our living space, energy level is still the number one challenge owners face. High energy is often the biggest driver of dogs' bad behavior. When a dog is young, their energy is the highest it'll ever be, but among working dog breeds there may not be a huge downward curve. These dogs are engineered to keep on ticking. Training will only get you so far, because even the best-trained dog in the world will have behavioral problems if it doesn't get the exercise it needs. I meet dogs all the time whose only "problem" is that they've got full tanks of gas and nowhere to burn it.

So how do you meet the energy needs of a dog who can outrun you by ten or even twenty miles? Get creative. If your dog gets along with others, the dog park or a regular play date where he can run it out with another dog works great. Running beside you (with you on foot or on a bike), hiking, fetch if you can convince your dog to retrieve—all of these are good physical outlets for your pup. I love weighted vests for working breeds because it wears them out twice as fast as just a normal walk. For any working breed or mixed breed with working-dog origins, an hour of vigorous exercise each day should be considered a minimum. Your dog will likely be willing to go in any weather, but if you live in an area where that's an absolute deal breaker once in a while, you might consider a treadmill designed for dogs.

Destructive Tendencies

This is a similar problem to energy overflow, but it has more to do with your dog's mental and psychological needs than the physical ones. Any breed in this chapter—any dog with a long history of independent work—needs mental stimulation almost as much as physical exercise. Many of these dogs are, in their own ways, crazy smart. Without activities that occupy their minds, they can develop aberrant behaviors and start to seem just plain crazy.

To make sure this doesn't happen, mix up the places you take your dog to walk or run so she can smell and see new things. Pick up a couple cognitive dog toys (like food puzzles) and put them on rotation at home so one always feels like a fresh challenge. Take an obedience class together and challenge your dog to learn something new. If at all possible, engage your working-dog breed (or mixed breed) in a dog sport. Agility, flyball, carting, dock jumping—there are a ton of these from which to choose. If you don't have the time or energy to do this yourself, consider hiring a dog walker to augment what you can manage. The small cost of getting a little help can save you a fortune in damage to your house and belongings if you've got a dog who simply needs more stimulation and less time to sit and think.

Need for a Leader

This is a breed group with big dogs, strong dogs, smart dogs, and dogs who've been entrusted to run the show in dozens of different ways over their history. They've been prized partners and companions of humankind. Today many of us are happy to just love our dogs, but remember that they earned their roles beside us by offering invaluable help with important jobs—keeping us safe, guarding our flocks, hunting with us and for us, and tirelessly doing hard physical work. These are breeds that were meant to confidently go about their business with a minimum of direction from people.

Working-dog breeds almost universally are at their most well-adjusted in homes where their owners are also confident, where it's clear there's a leader in the house. There are lots of ways you can fill that role, starting with teaching basic obedience and conditioning your dog until his responses to commands become proficient. A dog who has mastered this basic training knows who is the teacher and who is the student, and he has a system of actions that serve as fallback safety protections when he doesn't know what else to do. Before, during, and after you teach your dog, remember to reward good behavior and make time for play. Secure, well-behaved dogs don't obey their owners out of fear; they do it out of loving respect.

This is a group that thrives on having a strong leader. Without one, they may walk all over you.

Digging

Almost any dog can be a digger, but sled dog breeds are especially prone to this bad habit. Combine it with their propensity to run away and their ability to run for hours at a clip, and you've got the trifecta of a master escape artist. Dogs that dig come by this habit for the most logical and utilitarian reason: for centuries they'd end each day on the trail by digging down in the snow and tucking in for a few hours' sleep. Old habits die hard, and this is a problem I get called a lot about.

If you want to curb a digging problem, start by giving your dog a different outlet for her energy. Next, accept that this is a form of joyful expression for your dog, that her holes are her art project. So rather than trying to stop all digging, designate a space where it's okay for her to go to town and redirect her to that area whenever her urge to dig kicks in. You can even bury a toy to make it extra interesting.

For casual diggers or dogs who are just discovering it, one simple trick to discourage this bad habit is making your dog's project a whole lot less appealing to work on. When you poop-scoop the yard, put the droppings in the holes. Just like every other mammal, dogs prefer not to come into contact with their own excrement. This will not work on die-hard diggers, but if it's a passing phase for your dog, it may well do the trick.

Dominance

It should come as no surprise that in a group full of dog breeds created and honed to be outstanding at protection, there are some strong and deep-seated instincts to guard people, places, toys, and food. There are dogs in this group who will be especially wary of strangers, and dogs who aren't hesitant to let them know it with growls, barks, and dominant body language. This is one of the few areas where I advise against DIY dog training, because there's potentially too much at stake for both you and your dog. If your dog is acting dominant or aggressive, seek the help of an experienced professional trainer.

Great Examples

Belgian Malinois

There are four distinct Belgian shepherds in the herding group, but this one stands out for its relentless work ethic, deep intelligence, and powerful presence. These dogs are effective herders, but that's not what most of us know them for. Instead, Malinois fill some of our most sophisticated and demanding dog jobs. They guard the White House. They detect narcotics, accelerants, and bombs. They search and rescue. They are the whole package: powerful, smart, eager to work, and among the most notorious and capable dogs working today—and they're getting more so every year. Malinois are an example of a breed that's been substantially genetically altered in the modern day. They've been bred to be larger and more powerful than their ancestors of even just fifty years ago.

Mike Herstik trains Malinois as bomb detection dogs and for other high-performance jobs. Not surprisingly, he can't just hire a kid from the neighborhood to take care of his dogs when he has to travel. That's how I ended up taking care of Aryeh for a long weekend. Aryeh's a handsome, noble dog, but so tightly wound you can almost see the energy pouring off him. At one point I held up his toy from across the room, and he launched through the air and landed next to me, teeth on the toy, in a single, graceful bound in a fraction of a second. Aryeh translates to lion in Hebrew, and in that moment, this dog displayed all the strength, grace, and intensity of his namesake.

Owning a Malinois is kind of like owning a high-performance car that requires special training to operate, because they are bred to work and live to work. An average dog from most breeds sleeps more hours than it spends awake, but Mals are an exception. As one of the highest-energy breeds on the planet, they're never satisfied to lie low and do nothing. The upshot is that with very few exceptions this is a breed that is not necessarily recommended as a pet.

Boxer

The ancestors of today's boxers were mastiff-type dogs of war: massive and muscular with broad heads and powerful jaws. That intimidating form held as their history evolved and they became a premier European hunting dog, bred and trained to run down and hold giant game like bears and boars. As time passed, though, their function pivoted to pet life, and scores of generations of breeding have landed us at today's boxer—a trainable, loyal companion dog who can be great with families and is the single most popular working-dog breed. There's a catch: what hasn't changed about these dogs is that they still have powerfully high levels of energy. To be honest, in all my years of training, I've never seen a boxer get tired enough to run out of gas. And unlike many breeds that quickly outgrow their early high-energy stages, you can't expect a slowdown in a boxer until he's at least ten or twelve.

I've had two of these dogs of my own (you'll see Koda on the front cover of this book) and trained dozens of them. I love them, but they aren't a good first dog. There's an incredible learning curve with your first dog, and a high-energy breed like a boxer requires double or triple the investment of time, training, learning, and accommodating. They're an experienced owners' dog. I had this point driven home when a client—a well-known actress—brought home a boxer puppy and asked me to train it.

The puppy was adorable and a dream in terms of picking up commands, but I warned his owner one of two things was about to happen: either this dog was going to be getting a lot of daily exercise, or it was going to start doing a lot of damage around the house. This entertain-me-or-I'll-entertain-myself rule is somewhat applicable to all puppies, but boxers are among the ones that need attention and exercise the most. I recommended hiring a dog walker ASAP and setting aside a chunk of time to play with the puppy every day.

In between sessions of exercise, I recommended crating the

puppy so he'd learn to be comfortable being alone for short periods of time. Like many novice dog owners, this client thought using a crate, even under those limited and useful circumstances, would be cruel. Looking around the room, I was seeing rugs that cost more than my car, but I figured their preservation wasn't my problem.

Fast-forward a few weeks and my phone rings at 4 a.m. This was back in the days of answering machines where you could hear the voice message as they're leaving it. I let it roll to my machine and then heard the actress, inebriated and angry, sneering. "Brandon, you come and get this great white shark right now. Feed it to the lions. I don't care. What kind of dog trainer lets this happen?? I just got home and this damned hyena has eaten my bathroom. The rug, the cabinets, the door. . ." She rambled until she ran out of recording time, then called back to keep going.

In the morning, listening to it again, it was my turn to be furious. How long had that five-month-old puppy been locked in a bathroom?

That was my first question when I returned the actress's call promptly at eight, and when she did the math, she sheepishly admitted it had been at least eight, maybe ten hours.

"You realize he's not even capable of holding his bladder for that long?" I asked.

I went to her house one more time to check on the dog and reiterate the return on investment of a sitter/walker. The puppy was thankfully no worse for wear. The heavy custom-carved Italian door, though, was destroyed. If he'd been just a little bit older, his muscles and bite strength a little more developed, he would have made it out and had his way with the rugs.

This entire incident could have been avoided by meeting the dog's most basic needs. Despite the fact that they are an extremely high-energy breed, boxers are typically sweet-natured and loving with people. Meet their needs, and they'll be faithful, affectionate companions for life. Oh, and in case you were wondering, I quit working for the actress that day.

Saint Bernard

One of the world's original search and rescue dog breeds came into existence at a Swiss Alps monastery and hospice where feet-deep snow covers the mountains for as much as ten months out of the year. The hospice has been on the site for nearly a thousand years, but it was in the 1600s that the monks there bred dogs intended to guard the place. As it turned out, the Saint Bernard dogs were capable of a lot more than guarding. At eight thousand feet, the monastery was a rare spot where travelers could rest as they made the trek over the mountains, but getting to it was treacherous work. The monks didn't start keeping records until the early 1700s, but in the time since they did, these intelligent, gentle giants have over two thousand confirmed rescues of weary travelers lost or buried in the snow.

Pairs of these dogs did a job no human being could do—scenting the lost trekkers, digging down to find them, and then splitting up as one dog would lie atop the travelers to warm them up while the other one ran for help. The dogs were so efficient and effective in their role that when Napoléon crossed the passage with tens of thousands of troops at the turn of the century, the entire contingent safely made it across. Soldiers wrote letters and diary entries about the dogs who had saved man after man from dying on the mountains.

Today's Saint Bernard is still a brave but benevolent giant. These dogs are affectionate and loyal, but also often shy and stubborn. Thanks to their appearance in the Beethoven movies, they have been overbred for the past twenty years, with some breeders paying far more attention to looks than temperament. So even though the warm, protective nature of these dogs runs deep, they're not always saints.

More Working Breeds

Akita. Bear hunter. Samurai companion. Pit fighter. The Akita is a Japanese breed that's survived a long and sometimes violent history of seriously demanding jobs. These are imposing dogs—tall, wide, and heavy—known for their independence, strength, and quiet confidence. They can be testy with other dogs, and they are definitely not a good choice for a novice owner, but for an experienced owner willing to put in the time and training, this is a proud, powerful breed—one that's a symbol of loyalty and nobility in its native country.

Anatolian Shepherd. One of the dogs that can be traced back the farthest, this powerfully built breed originally hails from what is now Turkey. Dogs like the Anatolian are found in records going back to at least 2000 BC. One of the most remarkable things about these giant guardians is that they've remained largely unchanged over centuries of breeding. As one of the top livestock guardian dogs, in recent years they've become especially popular for their ability to guard a flock without bringing harm to any of the endangered predators that might come calling.

Bernese Mountain Dog. One of the cuddliest (and most distant) descendants of the Roman Molossus dogs that spawned new breeds throughout Europe, this breed originated in Switzerland and continues to work on Swiss dairy farms today. Berners are versatile workers, able to herd or guard livestock, pull carts and wagons, and easily fit in with families. Outside the working world, this breed has gracefully settled into pet life. They tend to be gentle, quiet, happy dogs, and as long as they get their exercise they can make great pets. The problem for these dogs and the people who love them is that their popularity has encouraged some questionable breeding practices, and the result is a breed that has way more than its fair share of health problems. They are plagued by orthopedic problems (including hip dysplasia), rare cancers, bleeding disorders, and heart conditions. If you have a Berner, be sure she's getting competent, careful veterinary care—her health will likely be the biggest challenge you face.

Bullmastiff. The bullmastiff's original role is long obsolete, but it still makes good use of the traits that gave it value. These dogs—crosses between mastiffs and bulldogs—were originally bred to protect English manors from poachers at a time when poaching was a capital offense. Bullmastiffs were bred to be territorial enough to recognize an intruder, brave enough to charge one, strong enough to bring one down, and controlled enough to restrain rather than dispatch him on the spot. The majority of today's dog owners don't worry too much about poachers, but we do worry about our families, and the combination of traits this breed has—strength, courage, dedication, and judicious use of power—makes them a frequent choice for families who don't want so much a guard dog for the family as a family dog who happens to guard.

Bullmastiffs—like all the mastiff breeds—need an experienced owner as well as a strong foundation of basic obedience training, but they can be loving family pets. Worth noting: this breed notoriously does not get along with other dogs or cats. They fit best in one-dog homes.

Cane Corso. This Italian mastiff breed traces its lineage back to Roman war dogs, and that legacy of intimidation is still visible today in these dogs' square heads, imposing frames, and the observant, confident attitude that presumes the dog has everything under observation and control. There's a legend that these dogs carried pots of flaming oil behind enemy lines for Roman soldiers, spreading flames and chaos. Whether or not that's true, it's a fitting story for a breed that commands instant respect. With training, corsi make excellent working dogs because they're born with enough drive and intellect to match their strength. With or without training, they're not a good starter dog, or even an intermediate dog. They're an expert's breed, capable of learning almost any task and being an excellent (but not cuddly) companion. These dogs nearly went extinct in the mid-1900s, but they're experiencing a resurgence today thanks to their tremendous potential as working protection dogs.

Doberman. The Doberman is the namesake of its original breeder, a German tax collector and dog catcher who wanted a smart, imposing, and protective dog to travel with him as he performed his highly unpopular job. During World War II, Dobermans demonstrated outstanding trainability, learning to respond to hand signals and to alert silently when they smelled enemy combatants. The breed was so well suited to the work that roughly 75 percent of combat dogs during the war were Dobermans. These dogs have reputations as badasses—one they've earned through their historical roles and reinforced by their taut and muscular frames, always-at-attention ears, and intense eyes. While they do best with owners who are experienced and comfortable being a dog's leader, Dobies' temperaments have been genetically altered a great deal from the intimidating and aggressive characteristics that once defined the breed. Most of today's Dobermans are friendly, sweet-natured, and loyal—and their keen intelligence makes them highly trainable. They do best with a regular schedule that includes long runs, trips to the dog park, or agility practice.

English Mastiff. The most popular mastiff breed is the ultimate gentle giant—a dog that can occasionally top two hundred pounds whose temperament tends to be more teddy bear than grizzly bear. The breed goes back at least two thousand years and through several dramatic turns of fate along the way, but the dog believed to have played the biggest role in the development of the uniquely English mastiff is one who holds a special place in British lore. On October 25, 1415, during one of the definitive battles of the Hundred Years' War, a vastly outnumbered British contingent prepared to do battle against French forces outside the town of Agincourt. The Brits knew they were at a disadvantage, but weather worked in their favor when French soldiers got mired in mud—turning their attempt to storm the enemy into a slow attack. In the course of the violence, a British nobleman named Peers Legh was gravely wounded, but his massive and deeply loyal dog stood guard over him through the day, keeping French soldiers at bay and only finally backing down when Sir Legh's own squire arrived. Legh didn't survive his injuries, but his dog's heroism became legend. The mastiff-type dog was returned to Legh's ancestral home, Lyme Hall, and she went on to become the matriarch of a line of English mastiffs that continued for nearly five hundred years.

Because of their massive size and power, these dogs were once used as guard dogs and for blood sports like bullbaiting and bearbaiting. By the early 1900s, though, their numbers in England were in decline, and they came to be known as butcher's dogs—presumably because in the lean times after World Wars I and II only a butcher could afford to feed such a big pet.

If you're wondering how it is that today's English mastiff is the kind of indoor dog little kids climb and families adore when it came from such violent origins, a good guess goes back to the 1940s, when they very nearly went extinct and were bred back to popularity. Today, in terms of temperament, these dogs can be borderline lazy, and they're one of the least demanding breeds in terms of exercise in the working group. A couple of leisurely thirty-minute walks each day should be sufficient for a mature dog. These guys are smart and easy to teach simple commands, but fair warning that most of them won't be interested in advanced training. This is a comparatively mellow working breed.

Great Dane. One of the tallest breeds at up to thirty-two inches, the Great Dane is a giant that draws immediate attention. Despite the name, the breed has no known ties to Denmark—it was actually bred as a German hunting dog. Hunting boar is hard, dangerous work—dogs and humans alike have been killed by them. These dogs—mostly slobbery and gentle today—once had to be a match for that kind of ferocity.

In the modern era, boar hunting with your dog isn't a common pastime (though there are dogs who are experts at it to this day). For the most part, the Great Dane has been reinvented as a lovable family pet. There's a big catch with these sweet animals, though, because Mother Nature never intended for them to be so huge. Until natural evolution catches up with their human-directed breeding, these dogs almost universally experience significant and life-shortening heart issues.

Great Pyrenees. These large, majestic livestock guardians are an ancient breed dating back thousands of years. Their shining moment in history, though, may have come when they were a favorite of the French royal court—so much so that Louis XIV titled them the "royal dog of France." They're beautiful dogs with thick white fur, sharp eyes, and a lot of brute strength to put behind their protective instincts. Even though there's some variance in temperament among individuals, they tend to be friendly with people and patient with children. Unlike most of the dogs in the working group, these dogs are still on the job and are commonly used to protect livestock. Those who aren't in the working world, though, are well adapted to being loved family pets.

Newfoundland. These dogs are born workers, though the last century of breeding has mellowed their temperament a lot. They have a long and storied history of toiling on fishing boats, but they've also earned their keep pulling sleds and carts, performing search and rescue, and serving as watchdogs. When Meriwether Lewis (of Lewis and Clark fame) set out on his expedition across the country, his most prized possession (and perhaps his favorite travel companion, outranking even William Clark) was his Newfoundland dog Seaman. The dog practically leaps off the pages of Lewis's journal with his feats of heroism. When the travelers were tired, he stood guard. When a buffalo barreled into their camp, he drove it away. When one of the men got in over his head while fording a river, Seaman dragged him to safety. When the expedition was out of food, this dog caught, drowned, and delivered game to their campfire—everything from squirrels to deer. Lewis received multiple offers for the dog in his travels, but Seaman was worth his weight in gold.

Even in a breed group with a lot of giant dogs, the Newfoundland stands out for its size. Males can get up to 150 pounds, and with their bulky builds and fluffy coats, they look every ounce of it. Despite their immensity, though, they're known for being not just gentle but actively engaged in looking out for their human companions. It's their sweet nature that defines these dogs more than any other characteristic. Some things truly can't be trained into a dog, and this is one of them.

Unfortunately, Newfies suffer from significant health issues, including enlarged hearts and orthopedic issues.

Portuguese Water Dog. Running up breed popularity lists since two of them lived in the White House, these distinctively mop-top-looking dogs served for centuries as all-purpose fisherman's helpers in Portugal before the rest of the world took notice. Historically, their jobs included untangling and retrieving nets, swimming between boats with messages, standing guard on ships in port, and even driving fish toward nets. A typical Portie weighs in at between fifty and sixty pounds—less than half the size of their water dog "cousin" the Newfoundland, but these dogs are still large and strong (just not giant).

Porties are typically sweet and playful, but they're also extremely high-energy dogs who are intelligent and can be willful. To meet their need for companionship and intellectual engagement, invest time in obedience training and reinforcing it. This is a dog who can learn not just the basics but also tricks and games. To meet its need for exercise, plan on a bare minimum of an hour of vigorous exercise each day, but more is better. This breed will likely never be a curled-up-at-your-feet pet, but these dogs can be great pets for families that can match their energy.

Siberian Husky. The husky is a dog in motion—running, playing, and digging its days away. Most of these dogs are friendly and outgoing, but they're not likely to moon around looking to you for affection or pining for your presence. A husky will love you, but asking it for devotion would be a stretch. Instead, this breed tends to have a bit of a love-the-one-you're-with mentality, and they're not at all afraid to get out into the world and make new friends. Like my friend's dog Lena, most huskies require beefed-up enclosures, and every one I've ever met requires a ton of exercise to be happy and healthy. They're bred for endurance (as opposed to sprint energy), and they can run for hours at a good clip—and that's the source of most complaints about their behavior. Because this breed has high energy, a strong prey drive, and a defining streak of independence, the best way to train them and make sure both owner and dog are happy is with consistency and routine.

Conclusion

The working dogs are an eclectic group with a colorful, consequential history—dogs that have played their part in both advancing and destroying civilizations. The working dogs were created to be protectors and helpers, and they tend to be powerful and independent. Some have more sociable natures than others, but they are all substantial, energetic dogs who are happiest when they have a purpose to fulfill.

HIGH-OCTANE SMARTY-PANTS: THE HERDING GROUP

In Chapter 1, I shared the story of an Australian cattle dog I rescued from a breeding facility. This girl was completely shut down and terrified of human contact—to the point of being unwilling to eat or drink. I had experienced trainers tell me the most humane thing to do would be to euthanize her. It's a good thing I'm a sucker for a hard case, because a week after her rescue, the dog I named Kirra was wearing a collar, taking treats from my hand, walking on a leash, finding her place in the pack, and looking to me for direction. She was starting to trust.

Kirra was also discovering her deeply ingrained herding instincts for the first time. As a dog who had never had a chance to run, I think she surprised herself the first time I turned her loose in the training yard. Like every herding dog before her, she looked it over, sized up the space, chose a direction, and set off to run the full perimeter. When she had done a lap, she stopped to sit beside me and survey her domain. Then she did it again. This behavior was pure herding instinct—taking stock of the space and taking charge of it.

Later that same day, Kirra hung out with my dogs Koda and Lulu in the living room. Koda moved to head out of the room, and Kirra butted up next to him and checked him with her open mouth—not a bite or even really the threat of one, but a pure herding move if I've ever seen one. Koda shrugged it off and went on his way, but Kirra was left utterly confused by her own action. She shut her mouth, sat down, tilted her head, looked at Koda, at me, at the floor, and back at Koda. If she could have spoken in that moment, I have no doubt she would have said, "Why'd I do *that*?"

Despite the stunted and neglected life she had led to that point, her true nature started coming out once she was given some patience and kindness.

———

Every spring, a cast of brave, buff runners shows up in southern Morocco for what's been billed as the toughest footrace on earth. The route for the Marathon des Sables crosses 140 miles of the Sahara over seven days. Entrants backpack their supplies—food, each day's water, sleeping bags, headlamps, and a variety of implements to help them get reoriented if they get lost in the constantly shifting desert landscape. Weather conditions are blistering hot in the day and starkly cold at night. The terrain is sand—underfoot, in shoes and eyes, and sometimes swirling violently in the air. The event is to runners what Everest is to climbers—the ultimate test of endurance. Since its inception, over twenty-two thousand competitors have run it to prove their worth.

And one dog, who just did it for fun.

In 2019, on Day 2, a medium-tall, lanky, brown-and-white, collarless dog got caught up in the excitement as a group of runners passed and he trotted in among them. There was a lot of chatter about where he came from, but nobody seemed to know. When he was still tagging along at the end of the day's twenty-mile leg, they dubbed him Cactus. Out of respect, they shared their rationed water and food with him. Out of concern, a runner who was a veterinarian checked him over and declared him healthy. For the next five days, this dog ran over a hundred miles, keeping pace with elite ultramarathoners who had been training for years. Day 4 is the most grueling of the race—a nearly fifty-mile stretch that runners are allotted up to thirty-one hours to complete. Cactus did it in eleven (in a sandstorm), unofficially finishing in the top 10 percent of competitors.

I've never met Cactus, but he's got the energy, attitude, stamina, and social inclinations that likely gave early agricultural settlers the revolutionary idea that maybe the dogs hanging around for scraps and shelter could be trained to manage their most valuable resource: livestock. Livestock guardian dogs had long roamed with nomadic herds, but as people reached the milestones of property, borders, fences, roads, and community markets, a new set of needs arose. We needed a way to get animals from point to point—to buy them, sell them, milk them, keep them safe at night, and let them graze in pastures in the daylight. There had to be a better way than doing all that work "by hand."

The Job Evolves

Today's herding dogs cover a wide range of breeds, from the mighty German shepherd to the laser-focused border collie to the vivacious and frequently comical corgi.

The trajectory that led to this diversity is one you can mark along a timeline of human history. As our agricultural sophistication and diversity grew, we devised more specialized dogs to be our helpmates. Each time we managed to domesticate an animal— sheep, goats, cattle, horses, even ducks—we bred and trained dogs to manage it, and those breeds adapted to the unique circumstances of their homes and flocks. And each time we set out to settle or conquer new lands, we brought our dogs. In many parts of the world, you can trace herding dogs from region to region across the map and end up with a tidy, logical evolution of breeds.

For example, in northernmost Europe (what's now Norway and Sweden), we know ancient spitz-type dogs lived side by side with nomadic tribes for thousands of years. Archaeological records suggest that these dogs resembled today's Norwegian buhund. The medium-build dogs evolved in the tundra, and it shows in their thick double coats, small ears, bushy tails, and tendency to carry a little extra body fat. During the two-hundred-plus years Vikings dominated not just their corner of the Scandinavian Peninsula but also neighboring regions they could reach by ship, their dogs helped shape modern herding breeds. Researchers believe that the Viking herding dogs played a genetic role in the Icelandic sheepdog (now known as Iceland's sole native breed), the Swedish vallhund, and the Shetland sheepdog (likely begun as a buhund–Scotch collie cross).

Key Traits

Hunters but Not Killers

One make-or-break herding dog trait is an arrested prey drive. These dogs need to feel deeply compelled to chase and control the movement of their flocks, but not compelled to kill them. It's not so much a trait that's bred *into* herding dogs as one that's bred *out*. The prey drive goes straight back to dogs' wolf ancestry, and it takes time and effort to engineer dogs who'll consistently do the work of following their instincts right up to but not over that line. Many of us have seen this dynamic in breathtaking live action. The first time your young adult dog spotted a squirrel, rabbit, cat, or even a smaller dog and bolted in hot pursuit, you probably worried. If she catches it, then what? Nobody wants that kind of chance encounter to turn into a violent scene.

Thankfully the vast majority of our pet dogs pass the test.

There's a good chance early breeders got a leg up in assuring this outcome thanks to the natural selection that led to the first domesticated dogs. Dogs inherit prey drive from their wolf ancestors, but even in a wolf pack not every animal is a killer. For the group to effectively hunt large game, some of its members head off and drive the prey, steering it to an alpha team that does the dirty work. Our ancestors likely deliberately chose dogs who played this role in group hunting to breed, just as they chose dogs who were receptive to paying attention to— and eventually taking direction from—human companions. It's a common misconception that a wolf is a wolf is a wolf, but in practice, individual animals play varied roles in a pack. Some are shy, some outgoing, some dominant, some submissive, some exceptionally intelligent or coordinated and some less so. You won't find a litter of puppies that are all identical or that are all alphas. That's one of the beautiful complexities of genetics. The wolf pack survives through a cooperative hierarchy that needs animals that can work together.

The psychological upshot of all this fine-tuning of instinct is prey drive that's curbed just enough to create a herding dog that circles a flock and brings them, under direction, to a leader, pasture, barn, or market.

Independent Thinkers

Throughout history, the ideal herding dog has been one that's well trained and obedient but also capable of making decisions and working unsupervised. There's a huge instinctual component to this that exists before training. Capable working herders understand and execute complex commands that have to be taught, but they can also step in as surrogates to their owners on many levels—displaying understanding of the tasks at hand.

Research into how many repetitions it takes different breeds to learn new commands shines a light on the unique intelligence of herding breeds. Border collies, for example, need only a handful of exposures to commit a command to memory. Some breeds require twenty, thirty, or more.

Highly Specialized

Even though dogs in the herding group have much in common, they're still a widely varied assembly. Many of their differences come down to the nuances of their jobs. If you have one of these dogs, chances are you've seen these instincts at home (though they come out in some weird ways when there's no flock to work with).

Herding dogs that evolved (with the help of selective breeding) from guardians diverged into two main areas of specialized work: herding and driving. Herders keep flocks together. Drivers move them from point to point (sometimes called droving when it involves trekking long distances). Some breeds excel at only one of these jobs; some are more than capable of doing both. Corgis, for example, are highly effective and energetic herding dogs, but their stocky body type isn't well suited for droving.

One of the most fascinating things in the world of working dogs is witnessing the differences in how these dogs go about their business. Classic herders move clockwise and counterclockwise around the perimeter of a flock to manage its location and movement. To move them forward, they approach animals from behind, chasing and even nipping at their heels to push the flock in a desired direction. When an about-face or U-turn is needed, they get ahead of the flock, adjust their direction, and then drive them forward. Watching a dog work this way—using a finessed mix of intense stares and overt and subtle body language to let a herd of animals know what's expected of them—will give you a new respect for the art and science of herding.

I've been training dogs all my life, and I can teach them to do (or not do) a thousand things, but you can't teach just any dog to herd that way. Trying to get a nonherding dog to work a flock with body language and eye contact would be like trying to teach a five-foot-tall kid to dunk on a ten-foot hoop or helping someone born with a low, gravelly voice to sing soprano. If the dog lacks the tools to do the job, there's only so far I can take them.

A good trainer can fine-tune these skills if the dog comes with the tools, for sure, but the wiring that causes a dog to get low and stare down a wayward member of the flock, silently warning it to stay within the fold—that's gotta be there from birth.

And while herders typically do most of their work at home, drovers were designed to take livestock to market and beyond. These dogs are capable of moving animals over long distances, keeping them in line (literally and figuratively) for miles and ensuring order along the way.

Built for the Two Big Es: Endurance and Energy

The most common and consistent characteristic that herding dogs share is their high energy level and the ability to maintain it. If I had to describe these dogs with a single word, "workaholics" is the one that comes to mind. Many of them would rather work than eat, rather work than sleep, rather work than play (because their version of "play" *is* work). These dogs were bred to work day in and day out. The fact that many have traded the wide-open spaces of farms and fields for backyards and patios doesn't change that one bit.

Behavior Challenges and Possible Solutions

SO MUCH Energy

Herding dogs have high-octane, long-life batteries. One trait that herding breeds carry from their ancient wolf ancestors and millennia of selective breeding is the ability (and desire) to be on the move. For a tender or a driver, this might translate to twelve or more hours on their feet and covering a dozen or more miles a day (even without ranging very far) as they keep control of their flock. For drovers, it's often even more and at an aggressive pace—all while staying mentally alert and in charge. Whether your dog is a purebred or a mixed breed with strong herding traits, she's got massive amounts of energy to burn, and getting that energy out will almost definitely be your number one concern.

Even the best trained dogs in the world will have behavior problems if they don't get enough exercise, social interaction, and mental stimulation. Keeping any dog cooped up is like never allowing a child to play. Keeping a herding dog cooped up is next level, like what happens when that child is a track runner with attention issues who's stuck in a chair by an open window on a sunny day. The scenario just doesn't work.

I get calls all the time from dog owners (of all breeds, but especially herding breeds) who tell me their dogs need to be trained because they're out of control. A substantial portion of these dogs turn out to be reasonably well trained but woefully underexercised. My advice on this is simple: sometimes you don't need a dog trainer; you need a dog walker. If your pet is an endurance herder, skip the walker and go straight for a runner. These dogs are ideal athletic training partners.

If you want an alternative where no one has to match your dog step for step, try a dog sport. Agility training, Frisbee, and flyball are all great outlets for your dog's excess energy.

And if you want to give your dog a true gift (and also see her do the work she was born to do), join a herding class and show her some sheep.

Destructive Tendencies

If we assess dog intelligence on a scale from one to ten (with one being dumb as a rock and ten being a canine genius), herding dogs consistently rate near the top. These dogs have high canine IQs. This is a good thing—most of the time. Because your dog is smart, he's capable of learning complex systems and tasks and being an intuitive companion.

Also because your dog is smart, he needs a way to engage his brain to be happy and mentally healthy. Without that, he may entertain himself by taking up chewing, digging, or otherwise wrecking parts of your home and yard.

Physical exercise goes a long way toward meeting this need because it introduces stimulation in the form of new sights, smells, feelings. Mental exercise will take your dog the rest of the way.

That engagement can come in the form of the dog sports I mentioned for exercise (those are two-for-one bargains for many dog owners), but it can also come in other forms.

Don't be afraid to get creative as you consider this task. I've trained dogs to do tricks, to play games, to participate in sports, and to help with jobs around the house. The task doesn't matter nearly as much as the outcome—an opportunity for your dog to focus his mind.

A good friend of mine who's a brilliant trainer likes to teach these dogs to find specific objects, like house keys. The novelty of getting the dog to find something that might actually get lost makes the process satisfying for everyone.

A Little (or a Lot) Obsessive

Dogs who use eye contact to control or direct their herds are especially prone to this one. When a working dog habitually gets hung up staring down a single animal or group of animals, herders describe the dog as "sticky." It's not a good thing on a farm, because a dog with a fixed eye is distracted from the big picture of the job. As pets, these dogs can get sticky, too, both in their vision and in their general behavior. When it happens in your house or backyard, it might just be quirky, or it may seem to border on obsessive.

Over the years, I've met lots of dogs with obsessive personalities, but herding dogs have presented some of the most interesting cases. One border collie couldn't seem to look away from an occasionally dripping faucet—not even to play or eat. After three days of watching the poor thing stare and whine, the owners called for help. Other dogs get obsessed with toys, keeping them constantly in sight or poking you endlessly with them.

These behaviors are often rooted in the dog not getting enough exercise, but sometimes they're just part of their unique and creative personalities. If the behavior isn't doing any harm, there's no need to try to correct it. If it's keeping your dog from eating or sleeping or being a good pet, though, you'll need to find a way to interrupt the pattern. For the sink-obsessed pup, closing the door to the kitchen did the trick. Other options included covering the sink with a beach towel and, of course, fixing the leak.

A Take-Charge Attitude

In an actual herding situation, a take-charge attitude is a highly desirable trait. In your home with your family, neighbors, and guests, it can be a liability. In the absence of a job and a clear role in the household, many herding dogs will assign themselves a position in the hierarchy and take charge of everyone they perceive as being beneath them (or, in some cases, everyone in general).

Once again, exercise and mental stimulation are factors, so be sure your dog has an outlet for his energy. Beyond that, though, herding dogs almost always want to know where they stand in the family org chart. You can make this a nonissue by providing consistent leadership. One effective way to do this is through obedience training. Teach your dog the 7 Common Commands (SIT, STAY, DOWN, COME, OFF, HEEL, and NO) and practice them frequently. If you want guidance in this endeavor, you can grab my first book, *Lucky Dog Lessons*. Since your herding dog is intelligent, add some additional commands to the mix. *Go to Bed* is a great one, and you can get double duty out of it by using it at mealtimes. When the dog spends your mealtimes waiting in a separate, quiet spot, it sends a clear signal that you are the leader of her pack. After all, alphas always eat first.

If you can give your dog confidence that the household already has a leader and clearly teach her which behaviors are desirable and which are unacceptable, you'll eliminate her power grabs, her confusion, and distress for both of you.

Chasing

Remember that at the core, every herding dog has a strong prey drive. That drive has been manipulated in a number of ways, but it hasn't been diminished. The number one stimulant for prey drive is movement. Just like any predator, a dog keys in on activity in general and running in particular.

The danger in this drive is that it's *so* strong that many dogs will heed it at the expense of all other intellect and logic. This is how dogs get out of the yard, how they get lost in unfamiliar neighborhoods, and tragically how they end up getting hit by cars. It's impossible to train this instinct out of a dog, so you need to manage it in other ways. First, work on the COME command until your dog has a reliable recall—and then work on it some more. With practice, answering your call can become more of an automatic response than a thoughtful choice, and you'll have a fair chance of keeping Rover from taking off. Second, secure your perimeter. Whether that means a fence or a long lead or closed doors, it's important to recognize that giving chase to any potential prey animal poses at least as much of a danger to your dog as it does to the animal he's after.

Nipping

This is one of the most common complaints I hear from owners of herding breeds. The simple answer is that in the absence of sheep or cattle to herd, your dog has surveyed the scene and chosen your children as a fitting substitute. Sometimes they choose birds, or tennis balls, or you, but kids are an obvious go-to because they're smallish, they make sudden and unpredictable moves, and they *run*. Some herding dogs can get their working fix by chasing the kids without doing any harm, but others sometimes go the extra step and employ their teeth.

If your dog has this problem, it's not much consolation that she came by it honestly. It's the luck of the draw if you have one that doesn't nip as much. I lose a lot of money telling people I can't train this impulse out of their dogs, but the fact is, you can't train an instinct into a dog, and you can't train one out. What you can do is institute control through obedience training. For a trained dog, a firm NO can dissuade bad behavior, and a reliable response to an obedience command like DOWN or COME can stop it and redirect the dog in the act.

If this is a bigger problem, you'll need to learn to anticipate your dog. Pay attention to what cues cause her to get nippy, and then head them off before she gets carried away. Knowing your dog helps you properly manage its behavior. Running is the most common trigger for this nipping, so teach children from a very young age that the best way to bring the dog up short is to *stop moving*. As soon as the herder stops perceiving one of the "sheep" is getting away, there's no job left to do. Also, while a lot of herding dogs' nipping is directed at the heels, sometimes this problem also crops up in the form of dogs nipping at children's faces. If your dog is doing this, odds are he's perceiving your child as a subordinate in the hierarchy who oughta be submissive. Teaching children never to get eye-to-eye with a dog, especially an unfamiliar one, is a good preventive measure, and so is routinely working basic obedience with the dog.

If you need help in this area, don't hesitate to call a trainer. They may not be able to eradicate an instinctive behavior, but they can likely teach you to read the signs and manage situations before they get out of hand, and they can most likely prevent this behavior from getting worse.

Critical Commands

Since herders are extremely high energy, basic obedience is always recommended. Be sure to put in extra time when teaching the DOWN command. This will give you control of your dog when you most need it. Also, teaching these dogs to HEEL can be more challenging than other breeds because of their genetics telling them to constantly move. For this I'd strongly recommend either a front clip harness (or a halter). It makes life much easier and gives you far more control on leash.

For advice on teaching DOWN and HEEL commands, please see *Lucky Dog Lessons* (details in Appendix A of this book).

Great Examples

Border Collie

Originally developed near the border of Scotland and England, the border collie breed is world-renowned as the quintessential herding dog. These dogs are so well designed for their purpose that they consistently rank among the smartest, fastest, most durable and capable breeds.

Breeding dogs is a complex long game, and throughout history it has led to unintended consequences—genetic shortcomings, behavioral deal breakers, medical conditions, and features and shapes that are less than ideal for a dog's functioning in the world. In the case of the border collie, it's fair to say breeders set out to create the ultimate herder and succeeded. That success translates into dogs that—like the first pup I ever saw herd sheep in Australia—don't necessarily need to be told what to do. They are born to the work, and the way they use their steps, their stares, and every muscle of their bodies to control livestock is a remarkable thing.

Of course, there's a catch. When an animal has been programmed over centuries to do one job enthusiastically and with minimal direction, it's almost impossible to separate future generations of those dogs from the work.

The combination of intellect, the need for exercise, and the drive to work can make these dogs a little quirky—or even borderline obsessive. Obsessiveness is a desirable trait in a herding dog with a flock to manage, but not so much in a family pet. Border collies' talents and needs can't be left at the door, so owners must find ways to engage them.

Two Aussies

Two breeds in the herding group have "Australian" in their name. One of them is uniquely suited to driving the toughest of livestock over the roughest of Down Under landscapes. The other, well, got their name largely by way of a little geographic confusion.

The first of these is the Australian cattle dog, and it is as tough and tenacious a breed as any on earth.

A friend of mine had one named Piggy—a name that suited her low, stocky frame and surprisingly short snout when she was a puppy. We took her to a herding class (yes, that's a thing—keep reading!). In the context of this course, dogs had the opportunity to test their instincts in a large paddock with a dozen sheep. For some of them, the opportunity to chase the flock around was a joyful but ineffective exercise. For others, like Piggy, it was a mission. The biggest challenge to the dogs who understood the rules of the game—encircle the flock, move them as a group, and get them all behind a small segment of fence—was a large, nasty-tempered ram that wasn't in the mood to play along. This guy was pretty much crushing the herding dreams of one novice dog after another. It started with a refusal to budge, then accelerated to angry grunts and threatening hoof stomps. The last straw was a brief but brutal attempt to trample a sweet sheltie—who made a beeline back to his owner, clearly not having fun anymore. Most of the dog owners were ready to pack it in then, but it was Piggy's turn. I guess our instructor knew the same thing about Australian cattle dogs that we did: they don't put up with any nonsense.

My friend gave the guy a nod and nudged Piggy forward. She was small but muscular, with a mottled gray-blue coat and a prominent patch of black fur around one eye. Her stance was tense and eager as she sized up the situation—paddock, farmer, ram, and sheltie. This dog only had a day's experience, but she clearly understood her challenge: all the animals were where they were supposed to be, except one. The ram raised his head to glare down at her, jutting his lower jaw forward to display his crooked teeth. Piggy twitched with excitement. Off leash and on command, she marched toward the ram until they were a short distance apart. They locked eyes like two gunfighters, each waiting for the other to draw—picture *High Noon* meets *Animal Farm*. The ram made the first move, lurching forward, but Piggy was faster and more certain of her plan. She charged him with all the force of a tiny, testy lion, leaped straight up, and nipped him on the nose. Shocked, the ram jumped back. The second it was in motion, Piggy began weaving back and forth at his feet, driving him toward the fence. The entire exchange was finished in less than a minute, and when it was over, the chastened ram was standing quietly with the rest of the flock, and Piggy was trotting back to us like she was ten feet tall.

This was a hard-core herding dog.

Early herding breeds managed sheep and other small livestock, but dogs like Piggy evolved over centuries to work bigger, rougher creatures. Given their size advantage, cattle are inherently more dangerous to dogs than sheep, and any mistake in their management has the potential to be deadly.

A dog who can stand up to that kind of power discrepancy has to be confident of its authority, so cattle dogs were bred to be mentally tough.

They are physically tough as well. Early ACDs were tasked with epic cattle drives over extreme terrain in the wide-open Australian landscape. They had to be equally sure-footed in the mountains and in the desert, and able to travel scores of miles every day—all the while keeping a herd of cattle moving forward in a cooperative unit.

It's no wonder that even today's Australian cattle dogs—often many generations from actual working dogs—have a reputation for being prickly. This was one of the few breeds I was told as a kid to steer clear of, but over the years I've found that most of the ACDs I see today seem to have been bred for sweeter temperaments than the ones I remember as a kid.

Of course some of the old curmudgeons may not be long gone, because this is a breed with the genetics to live an extremely long life. One of the oldest dogs ever recorded was an ACD named Bluey who lived twenty-nine years and five months—basically double the lifespan of the average dog.

The second Aussie herding breed, the Australian shepherd, isn't really Australian at all. These dogs have a uniquely multicultural history that originates in the Pyrenees Mountains between France and Spain, where the Basque people fine-tuned shepherds ideally suited to managing flocks of sheep in their high-altitude peaks. During World War II's labor shortage, American owners imported Australian sheep and enlisted skilled Basque herders to manage them. Records are incomplete, but it appears that some of these herders came from Europe with their dogs to join the sheep and others came by way of Australia alongside them. Somewhere along the way, both the humans and their dogs were presumed to be Australian natives. Much like the legions of immigrants who left Ellis Island with shortened and/or misspelled names, the Basque shepherd dogs picked up a new name and it stuck.

Once the ranchers and cowboys of the American West got a look at these dogs and their skills, they quickly adopted them as their own and continued to breed and train them. These beautiful, long-coated herding dogs have become synonymous with the Southwestern landscape and its working ranches. They continue to make capable herding dogs, but they've also made a successful leap into lives as household pets.

German Shepherd Dog

In the late 1800s, a retired German military officer in Alsace watched the native herding dogs working sheep and set his sights on breeding the ideal all-purpose working dog. In his lifetime, Max von Stephanitz honed a versatile breed that could herd with energy and precision; perform rescue, police, and military work; and still be a loyal, loving companion. Later, these German shepherd dogs would make history as the first seeing-eye dogs, cementing their place in another area of canine lore.

Not content to simply believe his dogs were outstanding, von Stephanitz wanted to prove it. He developed the basis for the Schutzhund trials that are still in use today (for any breed, not just German shepherds). These field trials are like decathlons of dog training—demanding that each participant demonstrate high levels of competence in tracking, obedience, and protection.

Over the years, I've had the privilege of working with countless German shepherds, and I've been blown away time and again by their intelligence, loyalty, steady temperaments, and seemingly unlimited capacity to learn. I've trained these dogs to be everything from family pets to service dogs, companions for the elderly to high-performing working dogs.

German shepherds are also a perfect example of an important trend that commonly gets ignored when we talk about dog breeds: the fact that there can be wide subsets within a breed. This isn't about individual differences (which always exist) but with generations of dogs, often with a shared region or job description, being bred to a different standard than others. Once this breed's popularity took off in North America, most breeders chose to skip the working tests—that standard was an extremely high bar and one that wasn't important to most families who were just looking for a pet. It was the beginning of a great divide, though, in the breed that persists today.

More Herding Breeds

Bearded Collie. Beardies are among the oldest herding breeds, originating in England to drive sheep and cattle. Even though these dogs were bred to be hearty workers, most have playful, affectionate personalities. With hair over their eyes and smiley expressions, these dogs always look like they're ready to have a good time. Worth noting that the coats on these dogs are a major commitment.

Belgian Shepherds. There are four distinct Belgian shepherds in the herding group, including the Malinois we looked at in the working breeds chapter. In theory, the Belgian sheepdog, Laekenois, Malinois, and Tervuren shepherds differ only in coat and color, but the AKC considers them four separate breeds. Bottom line is that all four of these animals are intelligent, muscular, fast, energetic dogs. Their unique combination of physical power and mental energy makes them ideal herding dogs as well as highly trainable dogs for almost any other job. What it does not make them is great house pets. These breeds are suitable for experienced, dedicated owners who can give them a job to do.

Collie. It's been decades since *Lassie* was a hit TV show, but the legend of the regal, loyal, smart, and heroic Scotch collie lives on in America's cultural memory. Even though our real-life collies live less dramatic lives than the dogs who played them on television, some things about the breed hold true. I don't doubt that these dogs still have the tools to be excellent herders, but very few of them are doing the work today. Perhaps because they're far enough removed from active herding to have lost some of their edge, these dogs make great family pets.

Corgi. The Pembroke and Cardigan Welsh corgi breeds are among the smallest herding breeds (their name roughly translates to *Dwarf Dog* in Welsh). The breed is believed to go back over a thousand years. Despite their size, corgis are effective cattle dogs—totally unafraid of the giant creatures they manage. They've also got a long history as guard dogs, in part because they tend to bark only when there's a good reason, and in part because they've been entrusted to play with and watch over children for centuries.

Old English Sheepdog. This is a drover's dog (not to mention the original Shaggy Dog). With their super-fluffy coats, lumbering gaits, and playful attitudes, it seems like this breed wouldn't be an effective herder, but in 1800s England, these dogs regularly drove whole herds of cattle to market. They may not have been the most versatile herders, but they were highly capable of moving big animals over distance. Around the turn of the century, the breed caught on in America in a big way—so much so that many of New York's most prominent families (think Morgans and Vanderbilts) took up breeding and showing them. It is worth noting that these dogs are not always the teddy bears they physically appear to be. The strength of both body and will it takes to drive cattle belies a powerful and temperamental animal under all that fluff.

Puli. In the world of dog breeds, none are quite as distinctive as this ancient Hungarian herder with its unmistakable corded coat that looks like dreadlocks. These dogs have a rich (if unconfirmable) backstory that dates the breed as thousands of years old and having traveled from ancient Sumer to Tibet to thirteenth-century Hungary, where they settled and proved so effective at herding that a shepherd could once expect to pay as much as a year's salary for a dog. Beneath all that fur lies a small, agile, affectionate dog, one of the rare choices among herding dogs that can acclimate to apartment life as long as it gets enough exercise.

Shetland Sheepdog. There are plenty of adjectives that get thrown around about herding dogs—words like energetic and powerful, clever and impressive. But you don't hear *gentle* very often. Shelties are the rare exception. These dogs are herders, but they somehow manage to do the job and be sweet about it. This is a breed that can herd ducks and toddlers. They make excellent pets.

Conclusion

The herding breeds are intelligent dogs bred to take direction. There's no group better suited to learning commands. These are high-energy dogs who can sometimes be obsessive. They require both attention and exercise. Without a healthy outlet for their intellect and energy, they will develop aberrational behaviors. With it, they'll be smart, loyal, useful companions.

FOCUSED AND FRIENDLY HUNTERS: THE HOUND GROUP

Every region has favorite dog breeds, like New York's French bulldogs and the burgeoning doodle mix population in California. In the Southeast, some of the most popular breeds are hounds, from the smallest beagle to the largest bloodhound. In 2018 I got a reminder of the unique charms and challenges of these age-old breeds when I taught a seminar at a southern shelter. I asked the staff to bring me a random dog from inside the shelter to do an on-the-spot training session, because throwing down the gauntlet of, *Just bring me a dog*, definitely keeps audiences engaged, wondering if I'll be successful. It keeps me on my toes, too, and (usually) proves the point that any dog can be trained to be made more adoptable.

The scenario that usually works out is how I found myself

standing on a stage in front of nearly two hundred people, watching as a shelter volunteer led a large, lumbering bloodhound my way.

Challenge accepted, I thought. I pulled out a treat and held it up, talking to the dog. He leaned toward me—drooling in the general direction of my hand. I was thinking I had him, that we were starting a simple, productive training session, when something shifted in the air. Whatever changed was imperceptible to me, but in that moment the dog picked up a scent he liked better than the treat. He turned his head, then his whole body, lowered his nose toward the ground, and began dragging the volunteer away.

I tried to recapture the big guy's attention, changing my voice and body language, but the dog had forgotten I was alive. He didn't want food, didn't want to see or hear anything while his nose was homing in on something interesting, and he definitely didn't care that the crowd was watching me step on this rake. I asked the volunteer to bring me another dog and she promptly returned with . . . a coonhound. The same thing happened. At that point, it was time to acknowledge the elephant in the room—the fact that when a hound locks in on a scent, even an actual elephant in the room might not be enough to regain his attention. Hounds can make loving and loyal pets, but thanks to thousands of years of breeding to ensure they're able to focus *single-mindedly* on following their finely tuned senses, they're not really training-on-the-fly types. This is why so many obedience trainers struggle when training hounds. They're in a league of their own, and a trainer typically has to specialize in hounds to get the best results out of them.

Does that mean they can't be trained? Of course not. These

are dogs who do extraordinary work in partnership with their people. The catch is that training a hound to do the work it was born to is nearly as much about allowing it to follow its instincts as it is about teaching it anything else. What that means today, when most hunting breeds never fulfill their biological destiny in the field, is that at a bare minimum you have to remember that your dog can't turn off its nose (or its hair-trigger impulse to chase anything that's running). Think about it this way: if you walk into a room that reeks with the stench of rotting fish, you can't just deny that your senses perceive it. Maybe you'll get used to it and block it out; maybe you'll have to walk away; maybe you'll cover your nose and carry on—but for a while that odor becomes the defining characteristic of the space and the moment. For your hound dog, life's like that all the time.

As for my seminar and its short-on-time training session, I had to ask the volunteer for a dog who was not a hound. She brought out a pit bull mix, and the rest of the seminar went smoothly.

Partners in the Field

Some breed groups only have loose connections tying them to one another, but when it comes to the hound group, they've got a bedrock trait in common: each evolved as a specialized hunter. Most of them were intended to work without the constant guidance of a handler, and many were bred to work together in groups. Thanks to their common purpose, these dogs have plenty of shared strengths and personality quirks, starting with the power of their instincts.

Hound breeds date back to the earliest human civilizations. In fact, even before dogs were working side by side with humans as our partners, we were undoubtedly scoping out wolves' abilities and using them to our benefit. We've been watching and relying on their superior skills to identify, track, and corner prey since the beginning of time. At some point we began a gradual shift from observing and maybe even commandeering their kills to harnessing their abilities by maximizing their tracking skills. It was the beginning of a partnership and survival adaptation between the two species. Over time we would purpose-breed hounds to specialize in every possible aspect of the hunt, fostering dogs that focus on specific species, dogs that could use their superior scenting abilities to find prey that was invisible to us, dogs that would corner their prey and wait, dogs that would dispatch it themselves, and dogs that would dare to target powerful and dangerous animals like bears or cougars—creatures that only became legitimate prey because of their partnership with human hunters. There's no great mystery as to where the origin of hounds' greatest skill lies—after all, prey drive is the wolf's ultimate survival instinct. The biggest distinctions in the hunting breeds that have emerged over time are in how they detect prey and how they pursue it: by sight or by smell.

The Sight Hounds

The earliest sight hounds—greyhounds and salukis dating back some four thousand years to ancient Syria, Egypt, and Rome—

hunted by eye and chasing speed. Even after all that time, your dog's vision is likely not as accurate as your own (if your dog wore glasses, they'd be bifocals with thin lenses on top and thick ones on the bottom), but dogs' eyes, especially those of sight hounds, aren't designed to do close work. These magnificent creatures— graceful, sleek, and aerodynamic—are perfectly engineered to detect prey. Both dogs and people have two primary kinds of photoreceptors in the retina—rods and cones. Our eyes are cone-heavy, allowing us to see well in daylight, to perceive infinite hues, and to be able to distinguish the distance between points. Dogs' eyes are rod-heavy, which makes them better able to see in low light and to be hyper-perceptive of movement. In other words, they may not be able to see all the colors in the vegetable patch, but if a rabbit comes creeping through the undergrowth, they're not going to miss it.

Sight hounds benefit from this extreme ability to detect motion, and they've also got one of the widest fields of vision of any canine. The positioning of their eyes gives them as much as a 270-degree field, meaning they can literally see not just what's in front of them and beside them, but to a significant extent what's behind them as well.

Great vision is one thing, but having it tied to a quick-thinking, fast-racing dog is what's made these dogs so valuable to human civilizations. Sight hounds can chase and catch prey that humans wouldn't have had a chance of overtaking with our own speed or primitive weapons. And they do it all while moving with such ease they look like they're floating on air. Thousands of years of breeding has done its job so effectively that every sight hound owner needs to be aware that their dog's bone-deep instinct to chase is still easily triggered by a fleeing cat or a scurrying squirrel.

Of course, even the keenest sight hound is still a dog, and that means the lion's share of its sensory perception comes not through its eyes but through its nose.

The Scent Hounds

The biggest question I get about hounds concerns their intelligence. If a dog doesn't listen or takes a while to train, people are quick to think they're not smart. But dogs, like people, have different kinds of intelligence, and there's really no better example of that than a scent hound. These dogs may take some extra time and effort to train because their noses can easily override their ears at any time (e.g., the story that opened this chapter), but what amazing noses they are. I'll admit scent hounds are definitely more of a challenge than some other breeds. Most of them don't become as well trained as a German shepherd, golden retriever, or border collie, but that's because their skill set isn't the ears, it's the nose. You need to roll with the punches and accept the fact that when it comes to training, not all dogs are the same. At their core, these hounds are brilliant real-life biosensors that have been outperforming human innovation and technology for centuries. At this writing, a hunting dog's ability to catch the edge of a vapor plume and follow it to its source remains something far beyond human attainment.

The way this happens is through your dog's superior scent-detection system. Their noses have hundreds of millions of scent receptors (far outnumbering what you or I have). Those receptors take up a disproportionate amount of space in hounds' long, wide noses. They also have a specialized gland called the Jacobson's organ near their upper incisors. It's a processing center for some of the most primitive types of smells—like hormones—and you can sometimes see your dog using it when he's got his mouth a little open, his head cocked, and that look of sensory rapture on his face—like *Are you SMELLING this?* The tools they are born with give hound breeds the ability to smell at least a thousand times more acutely than any man, woman, or child—and even that is likely an underestimation.

That kind of sensory intelligence may not be the stuff of obedience champions, but it's the foundation of every great scent hound's talents. First, they have to be able to detect their prey, and then they've got to run it down (or up, if they're a breed that trees their quarry).

Over the ages, scent hounds have been bred to help hunt all kinds of prey—from rabbits to raccoons, fox to elk, deer to bear, and even wolves.

Sight/Scent Combos

If you have a mixed-breed hound, don't be surprised if your dog displays both sight hound and scent hound instincts and behaviors. Not only do the two basic hounds often get crossed through natural pairings, but breeders have been deliberately combining them for centuries to create dogs that have both strengths. If you suspect that your dog has this kind of heritage, watch how she perceives new sensory input on a walk or at the park. Dogs with both kinds of hound in their blood may be equally likely to put their noses to the ground and take off sniffing as they are to catch sight of a bird or a butterfly and lock in, poised to run.

Key Characteristics

Even if you don't need your hound to hunt, things will go easier for both of you if you respect the thinking of the hunter. Taking your dog's instincts into consideration will make you a better owner, better trainer, and better friend to your dog.

One-Track Minds

The mind of a hound is amazing in its capacity to home in on a single objective to the exclusion of everything else. Hence the term *dogged*. Millennia of selective breeding have fostered this skill based on the logic that the fewer distractions the dog has, the more effective she'll be in pursuit of prey. For all intents and purposes, when these dogs are working, they're like missiles, programmed to pursue their prey accurately and relentlessly. We don't gum up our missiles by making them multifunctional, and as a general rule hound handlers have long considered obedience (beyond the basics) to be a distraction from their dogs' work.

Every facet of a hound's shape and senses ties back to its hunting function, from scent hounds' wide noses to the one wide feature on a sight hound—a ribcage containing its large and highly efficient heart. Total focus is awesome when it's directed at the task at which you want your dog to be successful, but it's not an advantage when his mind is on one thing and yours is on another.

Unique Pace

At first glance, it's obvious the sleek sight hound breeds are built for speed. Everything about them is aerodynamic and graceful, poised for motion. Scent hounds, on the other hand, often have more deliberate and heavy gaits and thicker body types (especially basset hounds and bloodhounds). It's true that most sight hounds will leave most scent hounds in the dust in a race, but there's an element of the tortoise and the hare in that comparison. Sight hounds are sprinters—capable of short bursts of extreme speed. Scent hounds are marathoners—capable of walking or trotting at a steady pace for hours on end. There's a strange irony to it when people adopt racing dogs as running companions, only to find that after a two- to ten-minute run (during which the human has zero chance of keeping up) the dog is *done* and ready to move on to the nap portion of the day. Meanwhile, most scent hounds would happily trot by your side all day and never complain or tire.

Going with the Flow

There are a lot of breeds and breed types that make a lifestyle out of laying claim to power. They posture, push limits, scrap among themselves, and vie for territory, all in the pursuit of being top dog. Among hound breeds, this is far less common and less extreme than in most groups. In a hound pack, the hierarchy is nearly horizontal, with dogs tending to work and live together cooperatively. Many of them don't care about being king as long as their basic needs are met. As a result, there's a good chance your hound or hound mix gets along with others both at home and in public spaces like the dog park.

Sound Matters

Most sight hounds are the swift and silent types, so much so that when they bark, they can sound a little raspy and awkward from lack of practice. Scent hounds are a different story. They can be crooners, barkers, or hair-raising caterwaulers—depending on your dog's unique circumstances and how you feel about the *roo-roooos* they make as they bay their hearts out. The way those distinctive tones can carry for miles is no fluke. The urge to bay—a sound somewhere between a howl and a bark—goes all the way back to dogs' wolf origins, when a howl was a multi-purpose tool that helped them protect territory (the ancient canine version of *Get off of my lawn*), and stay connected with one another even when they were far apart. Modern hounds' distinctive bay was developed through breeding, and the hunters who work them hear it like sweet music. The reason is simple: most hounds work ahead of their handlers—sometimes miles ahead—and the vocalizations that can be heard far and wide are the tool they use to communicate "status updates" from the front to the hunter in the back. Packs of hunting hounds also use their voices to communicate with each other, gauging the position of each dog as they cooperatively flush out or corner prey.

I've met plenty of hunters who can distinguish their hounds' calls from miles off, reporting on whether the dog is just catching a scent, in pursuit, or pacing at the spot where they've treed a raccoon, just waiting for the master to arrive. Without that steady flow of information, the hunter would have to keep the hound in sight—severely hampering its ability to do its job.

So some people love the bay and some hate it. Too often the latter group includes neighbors. The most effective step that owners of vocal hounds can take to ensure this isn't a problem is making sure your dogs aren't left unattended outside, where your lonely basset hound, beagle, or bloodhound may serenade folks for blocks around, whether they like it or not.

By the way, good luck to anyone trying to train a hound to stop barking on command. You'll probably die trying. I remember when I was young and coming up in my dog training business, I had a lot of clients ask if I could train their hound to stop barking on command. An inexperienced me said yes a hundred times only to fail . . . a hundred times. That taught me a powerful lesson at a young age. I had to learn that it takes a very experienced trainer to tell the client what is and what isn't possible.

Behavior Challenges and Possible Solutions

Need for Speed (or Distance)

After thousands of years breeding scent hounds that can run every day and track prey for long miles over any terrain, changing the rules to define a "good boy" as one that sits in the yard watching the clouds drift by really isn't reasonable. By that measure, good dogs are extremely rare.

Rather than trying (in vain) to turn off your dog's bone-deep, elemental drive to run, find a way to work with it. Create an energy outlet so he doesn't have to take matters into his own hands.

If you have a sight hound, the name of the game is finding a wide-open space for sprints (trust me, you will not be able to keep up if you try to run alongside these dogs). A fenced yard, the dog park, or even—*after* your dog masters a reliable recall—an open field. Most sight hounds will be over the moon if you encourage them to run by playing chase or throwing a ball or toy (but don't expect them to retrieve it because it's unlikely). Know that short bursts of speed satisfy these pups for long periods of time—a few five-minute sprint sessions every day will keep most sight hounds happy and healthy.

Meeting your scent hound's exercise needs will take more time. Figure a minimum of an hour of steady exercise daily to wear these guys out. Some dogs need much more. As you choose your routes, do your dog a favor and indulge in her desire to follow her instincts. Let her choose a couple of places to stop and smell the pavement or the fire hydrants or the trees each time you walk. To shake things up and really let her lean into her strengths, mix up your routes, visiting new places with new smells. Most scent hounds make cheerful, sturdy hiking companions who are willing to go as far as you like at your pace and genuinely happy to explore.

Almost any hound can make an excellent jogging partner. Being outside, trotting alongside you, seeing and smelling—that's their happy place.

High Prey Drive

Hound dogs have prey drive tattooed into their genetic code. They're likely to tune in to the sight or scent of any potential prey animal and get borderline obsessed. There's no way to turn off a drive that's been amped up through hundreds of generations of hunting dogs, so you need to be prepared to make judgment calls about what your dog can and can't handle in terms of stimulation. Some hounds simply can't live with cats, because they can't turn off the urge to hunt them. Some of them get along fine. Pay attention to your dog's body language and interactions with small pets (and even small children). A little curiosity and engagement are fine; however, incessant tracking is trouble brewing.

A simple rule of thumb here boils down to basic executive decisions all dog people must make. If you know your dog has heavy prey drive but lacks a solid recall, I'd probably forgo taking them to a park with lots of squirrels. If you can't successfully call them back to you when they're fully targeted on a critter, you might make things much easier if you hook them on a long lead while at the park. This way you have control when you need it. Now if your dog has the time of his life chasing critters at the park and it doesn't bother you—then let him free as long as it's a safe environment! Letting dogs indulge their prey drive can be a simple way to burn their energy. After all, they're just doing what their genetics are telling them to do—and there's no work involved for you at all.

Runners and Roamers

Hand in hand with their strong prey drive and breeding for independent work is the fact that any hound is a potential flight risk. These are dogs who run off at the slightest temptation, and I'm not sure I've ever met a beagle owner who can't attest that this struggle is real. I've met hounds who are climbers, hounds who are diggers, and hounds who will steel their nerves and deliberately blow through an invisible electric fence.

The first way to deal with this instinct is to provide plenty of exercise. Beyond that, though, know your hound is at high risk for taking advantage of off-leash moments and for exploiting weaknesses in your yard or containment system. Use a long lead, walk your perimeter, and get to know your dog's methods. Hounds are capable of learning a reliable recall—virtually any dog is—but you've got to make it a priority.

Hurt Feelings

Scent hounds often have stubborn streaks, and they require plenty of repetitions of their lessons before they sink in. It's just part of their independent personalities to not be especially concerned with what you want. They're geared far more to following their instincts than they are to taking direction. This is an area where scent hounds sometimes diverge from their sight hound brothers and sisters. Greyhounds, whippets, salukis, and other sight hounds are typically sensitive and affectionate creatures, super-attuned to volume, tone of voice, and body language. As a result, they don't respond well to discipline. These are dogs who require a gentle, balanced approach to training to do their best.

Work with your sight hound in small increments of time, and be patient, consistent, and kind. Use positive reinforcement to guide them. These dogs are intuitive and almost inherently polite, and they will learn enough basic obedience to be good pets with gentle guidance and encouragement. When it comes to their training, the Genghis Khan quote holds true: *An action committed in anger is an action doomed to failure.*

Condition, Condition, Condition

When it comes to training, you're always going to be competing with your hound's senses for attention and cooperation. Though generally sweet-natured, hounds were not bred to take direction from a handler. For centuries, they've simply been transported to hunting grounds and let loose to chase down their prey. Because of this, they pose unique training challenges. Sometimes you'll win because you guys are buds and you're putting in the work. Sometimes you'll tumble down the list of priorities as his nose or eyes take the lead. The only way you're going to be able to trust that your hound's basic obedience is reliable is to condition each behavior until it happens on autopilot. The crux of this is training in short, frequent sessions multiple times each day over a matter of weeks. In the beginning, reward success with your dog's favorite treats, and over time offer those rewards less consistently. Just like people, dogs form habits as their brains create new pathways. There's no exact number of repetitions that's a sure thing, but about three weeks of routine training is a good guideline to get your dog to the point where he doesn't have to think about whether to respond to your request to SIT, or COME, or STAY, because doing those things will become automatic instead of considered reactions.

Remember that your training goal is always proficiency. I can teach a dog to sit in about a minute, but getting that same dog to proficiency, or more importantly reliability, takes a few weeks of steady, positive work.

A Wandering Nose

You can't change the fact that your hound will be easily distracted by new or interesting smells (or anything moving if you're dealing with a sight hound). At times, a scent will transport her, quite literally, to another world—one hundred yards, five hundred yards, or even a mile away. What you can do during training time is give yourself an edge with one simple action: start your training inside. No matter what you're trying to teach your pup, you'll be competing with far fewer random smells and sights indoors than in an outdoor setting. As your dog gets the hang of responding to a command, you can expand into environments with more distractions.

Take it step-by-step: First establish a clear understanding of a command and the response that is expected. Then practice for consistent proficiency. Then work up to a reliable response under distraction.

The #1 Command

Because most hounds are easily caught up in the moment and capable of traveling miles at a stretch, they're prone to running off and getting into trouble. In addition, their independent nature often means they aren't in the habit of constantly checking in with their owners for guidance or reassurance (like a lot of sporting and working dogs do). All this means that the hunting breeds more than any other group must master a reliable recall. Teach your dog the COME command right from the beginning, and do it so thoroughly and often that coming when called becomes an automatic conditioned response, not one he has to think about.

Whether you've had your dog for a day or ten years, if you haven't already done this, start now. Don't worry too much about teaching your dog to come from a sit or a down. Instead, work on getting him to come at random times and in random situations. Do it throughout the day and be prepared with a favorite food reward. When you're introducing this concept, don't ask your dog to go through a repertoire of obedience exercises when he gets to you. Just let him come, get rewarded, and hear nothing but encouragement in your tone. Practice in different rooms, from other people, and then outside, where there will be distractions ahead (because a hound can *always* find a distraction). Use a long lead and praise your dog as soon as he starts to make that U-turn back toward you when you give the COME command.

The most important thing in teaching this command is ensuring that your dog feels good about obeying it, so teach this skill with black-and-white clarity. Coming when called is always a positive experience. Remember, the secret is to make it so simple he can't help but understand.

Great Examples

Bloodhound

In June 2020, a New Jersey bloodhound named Blue and his handler arrived at the home of a missing child. The little boy had been gone for hours, and now it was 11:30 at night and his parents were terrified. Law enforcement vehicles lined the street and neighbors walked from house to house, calling the child's name. Blue put his nose to the boy's pillow, then lowered it to the floor. With his handler in tow he marched off the porch, around to the front of the house, and down the street. Four doors down, he veered into another family's yard, breezed past the house, cut a straight line to a tree at the edge of the yard, and sat down next to a sleeping child.

Problem solved—and a happy ending for a heroic search and rescue.

Of all the divergent hunting specialties hounds have developed, bloodhounds are unique for having become skilled and remarkably reliable people-hunters. Their road to earning their unofficial nickname of sleuth hounds is a long and winding one.

The forebears of today's bloodhound are History Channel–worthy characters. Those hounds date back over a thousand years to a French monastery called Saint-Hubert, nestled in the hills near the Belgian border. In keeping with their namesake's title as patron saint of hunters, the monks established one of the first documented dog breeding programs in human history. Thanks to a uniquely medieval "outreach program," they had a hand in boosting the popularity of hounds all over Europe and in creating many of the breeds that still exist.

Each year the monastery gifted a few pairs of St. Hubert hounds to the French king, and he in turn made a habit of sharing those dogs with favored subjects and other royalty. There's nothing like being a royal present to raise the cred of any dog breed, and the hounds (and hunting with them) gained popularity over centuries and across the continent.

Lots of unique hound breeds ensued, but the closest breed to the original is the bloodhound. These big, burly, energetic dogs with gifted noses excelled at finding wild boar and flushing them out to packs of smaller dogs. They were maybe a little too good at the job, because boars began to go extinct in England and then across wide swaths of Europe. Awesome as they are to this day, extinction of their prey could easily have been the end of the bloodhound themselves.

Today bloodhounds remain the ultimate scent hounds, but that's not what most people want them for. We like their big sad eyes, their long soft ears, and the determined way they carry themselves, but anybody who's ever trained these dogs can tell you they need a lot more out of life than a shady backyard and a cozy spot on the couch. In fact, a lot of bloodhounds end up in professional training after they don't get what they need as family pets. I'm not saying these dogs can't make great pets, but it's critical to accept that bringing one home is a commitment to honoring a long legacy.

Dachshund

Dachshunds are the smallest of the hounds, and because of their size and ability to be tenacious in working underground, odds are they've got terrier blood flowing through their veins in addition to their hound origins. Their German name means "badger dog," and in fifteenth-century Germany these guys were aggressive, effective hunters—dogs that definitely did not fit the image of the adorable "wiener dogs" we know and love today. If you have a dachshund or dachshund mix, that badger hunter is still in there somewhere, and it comes out in the feisty, brave, and sometimes willful personalities of these small-size dogs with gigantic character.

My own experience with dachshunds will forever be marked by a near-disaster outing in a park in the Pacific Palisades. I had arrived with my client's two miniature dachshund puppies,

George and Gracie, who needed practice coming on command and were ready (or so I thought) for off-leash work. Everything was going great until one of the dogs caught a whiff of the ground squirrels whose dens tunnel under the park. The den openings were wide (likely because coyotes had been scouting them), and while George was running to me for a treat, he veered off to the right—and disappeared into one of the holes. Gracie was right on his heels, and just like that I was down two dogs. I raced to the hole and poked my head in, but I couldn't see far and it was clear that wherever the dachshunds had gone they were out of reach. I heard a bark echo up from another hole and ran to that one, jamming my head underground and using the flashlight from my phone to illuminate the tunnel below.

Nothing.

There's not much in a training situation that can cause me to panic, but this was getting worse by the second, and my stress level rose with every hole I checked and every time I bellowed these dogs' names into the earth. My clothes, hands, and head were covered with dirt, but I was fixated on the call I'd have to make: *Your dogs are fine, but they're three feet under the park and I'm not sure when we might see them again.* The thought of that humiliation kept me searching instead of dialing. I hunkered down over yet another hole and poked my head in the entrance, and that's when I felt something goose me from behind. I looked up, and there were the two missing dachshunds, sniffing my butt.

That was the end of off-leash training for the day. We were going back to long-lead training until they earned another chance.

Greyhound

I had a client who wanted to film her greyhound running off leash, so we went to an enclosed park and positioned a drone capable of flying at 35 mph above and fifteen feet in front of the dog. With everything in place, the owner went to one end of the park to call Axl and I stayed behind to turn him loose and man the camera. The owner called, I let the harness go, and this dog was *gone* at a pace somewhere between galloping and soaring. I had the drone zipping across the sky, but even before I downloaded the footage I knew what we were going to see: a half-second streak of dog and then nothing but grass and dirt as the drone tried and failed to keep up.

From the time of the Egyptian pharaohs, a version of the greyhound has been revered for its grace and speed. Unlike some breeds that have been altered to the detriment of their health or temperament over the ages, thousands of years of fine-tuning greyhounds has achieved a dog that's the canine equivalent of a Lear jet: sleek, strong, graceful, and beautiful. They're also quiet, clean, intelligent, and not prone to any major genetic health problems.

When you look at the greyhound (and many of the other ancient sight hound breeds), they are the sum of features that contribute to their speed. They're muscular, with less than half the body fat of other breeds their size. Their bones are light. Their feet are long, narrow, and sturdy. Their heads, necks, trunks—essentially every individual part of the whole—are streamlined and aerodynamic. And when they launch out at speed, their extremely long back legs swing out in front of their entire bodies, propelling them forward with a highly unique double-suspension gait—the same efficient, powerful galloping movement used by cheetahs and antelope to cover ground at astonishing speeds.

They're also friendly dogs, typically with peaceful and affectionate personalities. It might seem like this breed would be an ideal running partner, but in this case two plus two does not equal four. The running dog doesn't actually make a good running partner, because it's good for a blisteringly fast half mile or so, and then it's back to the sofa for a long, restorative nap. Experienced greyhound owners know this breed is actually extremely mellow for most of the day.

Rhodesian Ridgeback

Among the hound breeds, none was developed to be skilled in pursuing a more intimidating adversary than the Rhodesian ridgeback. For the century or so these dogs were fulfilling their original purpose, they were southern Africa's premier lion hunters. Ridgebacks worked in packs, detecting and chasing their deadly prey. They would harass and distract a lion to keep its attention off the human hunter. It was perilous work, and a lot of these beautiful dogs lost their lives doing it. Most people would think a lion hunter would be the most aggressive breed in the world, but they're far from it.

What kind of dog does it take to embrace the challenge of pursuing the king of beasts? As it turns out, it's a breed with a lot in common with the lion itself. Ridgebacks are large (up to a hundred pounds), heavily muscled, sleek, gorgeous animals, instantly recognizable by the definitive cowlick ridge of fur that grows along their spines against the rest of the coat. Their manner is confident, dignified, and intensely loyal. They're quiet dogs, not prone to making a fuss without good reason. Everything about the way they carry themselves exudes understated but unmistakable power. The unique combination of these qualities is the result of crossbreeding the ultimate sight hound (the greyhound) with a large scent hound (genetic analysis suggests the bloodhound), and the fierce native guard dogs of the Khoikhoi people of southwestern Africa.

Ridgebacks are a fairly rare breed in the US, but if you see one you'll know it (and it'll make an impression). When I was training animals for movies and television, we had one ridgeback in our dog pack. His name was Odin, and he was everything a dog that's the namesake of a Viking god should be: regal, powerful, and benevolent unless you pissed him off. The thing I remember best about Odin, though, was that even though he had never seen a lion in his life, he was constantly and inexplicably drawn to their enclosure. Dogs and lions were on opposite ends of the ranch, deliberately positioned so that they would never encounter each other. When I walked other dog breeds in the general vicinity of the lion enclosure, they seemed to smell danger and always kept their distance, veering a few steps away where they could. Odin, though, was drawn to it. On leash, he'd pull toward the fence that hid the lion enclosures. He'd pace or make a show of trying to dig in that direction. He'd cock his head and focus his gaze straight toward where his genetically determined prey was hidden, his entire body at attention, as if to say *There's something over there I need to see.* I'm certain he had no idea why, but his natural attraction to the scent of the lions is just one more reason I've learned to respect the fact that long-outdated genetic impulses run incredibly deep in our domestic dogs.

More Hound Breeds

Afghan Hounds and Salukis. These similar sight hound breeds have a lot in common. For starters, they're ancient, revered, and culturally important dogs whose own histories are closely entwined with their regions (Afghanistan for the Afghan hound, the Middle East for the saluki). Both were the companions of ancient kings. They're tall, lean, elegant-looking dogs with dignified, quiet temperaments. These breeds (and mixed breeds including their DNA) aren't known for being obedience champs, but that doesn't mean they can't be well-mannered. Most of them are gentle, loyal, and easy to coexist with. Breeds like this are a good reminder that "obedience" as a concept that includes all the basic commands we expect dogs to respond to today really didn't exist until modern times. Not being quick to conform to the fairly new norms of learning to obey the 7 Common Commands is no reason to write off a dog's intelligence or fitness as a pet.

Coonhounds. Once upon a time, European settlers in North America brought their premier hunting dogs—foxhounds—along to help them conquer New World wildlife. They quickly discovered that raccoons, bobcats, opossums, and even some bears could easily disorient or flat-out lose their pursuers by doing what came naturally—climbing trees. With that in mind, coonhounds are America's answer to the foxhound problem. These breeds aren't exactly alike in appearance or temperament, but they share a talent for hunting by treeing.

Coonhounds are super athletic and high energy, but once you meet their exercise needs they're happy to pal around with you or with other dogs. Unlike some breeds that have been substantially changed over the past thirty, forty, or fifty years to make them more suitable as house pets, most of these dogs are still genetically similar or even identical to their working peers. They have strong instincts to seek, chase, and corner prey. These are highly coveted traits that hounds have been selected and bred for. Nothing you can do in your dog's lifetime is going to change that, so be prepared to work with it instead of against it.

Basset Hound. The basset hound, like the bloodhound, is believed to be traceable back to French St. Hubert hounds. In their case, the objective was to create a breed with a powerful nose and strong tracking instincts—but one that would move at a pace a hunter could match on foot. In French, *bas* means *low*, but it might as well have also meant *slow*, because that's what breeders were after. Bassets can be lazy, and they can be stubborn, but they're motivated enough by food to help you overcome any challenges that come up because of that combination of traits. Since these dogs are prone to a host of potential health problems, make a point to give yours plenty of exercise to help it stay fit. Nothing about these dogs is lean, but you do want to keep yours strong.

Beagle. Beagles consistently rank among the top three favorite breeds in the southern US. Part of that is attributable to a long history of families having working hounds. Part of it is because they're right-size and adorable (note the wide-eyed beagle stare—it's like they invented begging). Part of it is because, well, Snoopy.

These small hounds were bred to hunt rabbits, but today most of them are pure pet. They're friendly, gentle, cuddly, and usually happy to get along with other dogs and with kids. Of course nobody's perfect, and these dogs are just as happy to make friends elsewhere as they are at home—they're natural rovers, cheerfully wandering off to see the world whenever they see fit.

The fact that you're more likely to find this breed snuggling with the kids on the couch than working the land with a hunter doesn't change the fact that beagles have incredibly capable noses. Even though they're smaller than their cousins the bloodhound and basset hound, their sense of smell is nearly as acute. The combination of cute and capable has made them the darlings of the US Department of Agriculture, which has a 120-team-strong Beagle Brigade working at airports across the country on any given day. Part of the reason the department chose beagles instead of one of the many other breeds capable of doing the work is that they're just not intimidating. That puts travelers at ease, and the dogs can go about their business of detecting smuggled food products without disturbing the peace in the airport.

English Foxhound and *American Foxhound*. Sure, it seems obvious that these breeds were created to hunt foxes in the English countryside (and later, the American one), but their main function was actually hunting deer. Getting rid of foxes, which can be a menace to any barn or henhouse, is just the sideline that got them their name. Foxhounds have a long and aristocratic history in England, plus an impressive commoner history in the US. You're not likely to encounter either of these breeds very often, but if you're considering one, remember that like the coonhound breeds, these are dyed-in-the-wool hunters who need opportunities to walk, run, hike, and use their finely tuned noses to truly be happy hounds.

Irish Wolfhound. If you meet one of the giants, you'll remember. A friend of mine's toddler thought his first wolfhound sighting was of a horse. These dogs have been part of Irish lore and life since at least AD 300, and in going on two thousand years their function has changed from a massive sight hound skilled at hunting big game to a guardian against wolves to an emblematic representative of their culture and big beautiful dogs everywhere. The progression of those jobs was a risky one, because as each prey species went extinct, the hounds' presence in the Irish countryside became less necessary. After all, who needs a wolfhound when there aren't any wolves? By the early 1800s, the breed was fading into the country's history, but a Scottish army captain made it his life's work to bring them back to prominence. Today these dogs are a source of pride for Ireland and everyone who owns one. Despite the fact that they require a commitment proportionate to their size (they poop like horses, too), they're a popular and beloved breed.

Their size, bearing, and even their name make these dogs seem like mythical beasts, but the fact is they're more teddy bear than monster. They're gentle, friendly, and renowned for their loyalty. They're heartbreakers, too, because this is a breed that typically lives just six to eight years.

Whippet. Some historians say these dogs were bred to be a "poor-man's greyhound"—small-size racers developed by miners in northern England. Some say they're the result of crossing greyhounds with terriers—a recipe for a super-fast ratting dog. I think of them as elegant little catlike dogs—gentle, clean, quiet, and always looking to settle in for a nap in a warm, soft spot. Whippets are far and away the fastest breed of their size, but like their bigger sight hound cousins, they're short-burst-of-speed runners, not long-distance athletes. They need opportunities to run to be happy and healthy, but they'll take them on sunny days, thank you very much. Unlike most of their hound brethren, these dogs don't like to be wet or cold or muddy. They also don't like to be lonely—as true pack animals, they get very attached to the other dogs, kids, and family members in their households.

Conclusion

Scent hounds are active, physical animals with strong drives. They're bred to be vocal so that they can be heard during the hunt, but this admirable trait in a hunting dog does not always fit well in an urban setting. Sight hounds are their quiet counterpart—not to mention the epitome of grace. A hound's single-mindedness will be your biggest training challenge, but it's one you can work through. Most hounds are otherwise sweet-natured, sociable animals—ones who happen to require a lot of exercise.

HUNTERS WITH HEARTS OF GOLD: THE TERRIER GROUP

If you knew me circa the early 2000s, chances are you knew me with a Jack Russell terrier by my side. Pepe, whom you met in the introduction of this book, went everywhere I went—my dog-shaped shadow. He had a huge personality—fearless, feisty, extremely smart—basically a twelve-foot-tall dog in a twelve-inch-tall package. True to his breeding, Pepe's most joyful moments were spent chasing squirrels.

This was a dog who had prey instincts tattooed in every cell, and one day I swear it cost him at least two of his nine lives. That morning, we were at a park near the California coast, and Pepe was in his glory—running squirrels up trees and barking after them like a madman. I guess it was just a matter of time before one of the squirrels tried to even the score. The rodent went racing up a tree with Pepe at his heels, and what happened next was one of those moments you see in slow motion for the rest of your life: the squirrel long-jumped from one tree to another, and Pepe hurtled after him—missing both trees and then soaring over the park's boundary fence and out of sight. I ran up to retrieve him, but beneath where my dog had just taken flight there was nothing but a steep cliff dotted with thorny shrubs. Worse, at the bottom was a bustling road. And there was no small dog on that bank—an ominous sign.

It takes a lot to rattle me. I've worked with wolves, tigers, bears, and dogs of all sizes and temperaments. I've been bit, scratched, growled at, and tackled—and usually managed to keep my cool. But that day? I was terrified for my dog. I jumped in the car, sped down to the lower road, then started scrambling back up the nearly vertical embankment, calling Pepe's name and peering into every spot big enough to camouflage him.

The longer I looked, the more worried I got. I knew he could be lying on that slope or under one of the bushes, wounded or worse. But it was as if he had vanished. When I finally got back down to my car, dirty from head to toe, I was stumped.

And that's when a guy walked up from the beach to tell me he'd seen a little white dog get into a car . . .

My first thought was, *He's ALIVE!* My second was, *Man, where were you while I was crawling all over that cliffside?*

Back at home, I called animal shelters and veterinary offices. I made flyers and enlisted friends to help distribute. In less than twenty-four hours, we had found my dog, alive and well and miraculously uninjured. As I pieced together the story, it came out that Pepe had, indeed, sailed over the cliff and wound up on the busy road. What I hadn't seen was the passing driver who spotted him, pulled over to the shoulder, opened the car door, and called, "Here boy!"

Pepe was no dummy. He raced over, hopped in, wagged his tail at the stranger, and kissed her on the face. Then he settled into the passenger seat for his next adventure (which must have disappointed him because it was straight to the closest veterinary office).

There are precious few dog breeds with the kind of amped-up prey drive terriers possess, and that day mine proved that even though these breeds are known as *earth dogs* (the root of *terrier* means *earth*) for their willingness to go underground to catch their prey, if conditions are right and they're sufficiently fired up, they're also willing to try to fly.

Truth about Terriers

Most people choose their dogs based on looks—size, shape, cute eyes and ears, wagging tail, soft coat—and many do it without taking into account the history of the breed and how that might make the dog a great fit, or a constant struggle, with their lifestyle. No breed group brings more surprises in this area than the terriers. Most of the classic terriers are smallish and adorable, with sweet faces and plenty of positive energy. What you can't tell at a glance is that these dogs were bred to be relentless and deadly hunters. Even the cuddliest Westie or the most dignified Scottie can trace its family tree straight back to a time when its ancestors were the most effective extermination system in the world.

These animals are the earth dogs, not in a tree-hugging way, but in a burrow-underground-and-solve-your-rodent-problem way. The vast majority of terrier breeds were first developed in the British Isles, starting more than four centuries ago, to keep farms and homes free of mice, rats, and sometimes bigger pests like groundhogs, badgers, and foxes. It's impossible to overestimate the value of this work at a time when small farms were the norm and every cache of stored grain was an infestation waiting to happen. Rats were a scourge on many levels—consuming grain needed for livestock, contaminating what they didn't eat, and carrying diseases. They were difficult to eradicate, too—because they're big enough and mean enough to pack a nasty bite.

Terriers, bred to instinctively detect and dispatch vermin on automatic, were the answer to the problem. These dogs provided a prized service, and some of them still do. Case in point: in 2020, a group of eight terriers was brought in to get a British farm's rodent infestation under control. Over the course of a single workday, these dogs found and killed a staggering number of rats—over seven hundred of them. Total decimation. If these were big dogs, we might be afraid of them; but as it is, they're very much man's best friend.

Wondering what big hairy monster breed could do that kind of damage?

They were Norfolk terriers—ten-inch-tall bundles of fluff and muscle that look more like Paddington Bear than any predator I've ever met.

Over multiple centuries, regions and even individual farms developed their own unique versions of the dogs in this group— some shorter or taller, some leaner or more boxy, some built for speed and others for strength. They were chosen for color, for wiry or smooth coats, for their scrappy temperaments, and for being utterly fearless on the hunt. Many of the other dog breed groups have histories all over the globe and world timeline, but most of the terriers—including the Border, Skye, West Highland, Scottie, Bedlington, Irish, and Jack Russell—originated in small, distinct regions and sometimes even on specific farms and estates in the British Isles.

Even though terriers' origins trace back to work, by as early as the mid-1800s they were becoming something more than the help. They were prized possessions, sporty companions, comical sidekicks, and just snuggly enough. When prominent members of society started putting these dogs on pedestals, the era of them being indoor pets began. At the turn of the century, Britain's King Edward VII famously had a wire fox terrier named Caesar who had his own footman. In the early 1900s Rudyard Kipling published stories and poems about his Scottie; and by the 1930s glamour days of Hollywood, terriers were the kind of hot companion to movie stars that Chihuahuas would become seventy years later when *Legally Blonde* rolled around. Cary Grant, Bette Davis, Joan Crawford, Humphrey Bogart, Jean Harlow—they all kept terriers and were frequently photographed with them. Pretty soon everybody wanted to have one of these small, sturdy, spirited dogs.

It's been close to a century since owning a cute little terrier became a cultural phenomenon, and demand for these dogs as pets definitely influenced their breeding, but in many ways the group has remained true to its origins—energetic and independent-minded hunters who are scrappy to their core. When Mark Twain wrote "It's not the size of the dog in the fight, but the size of the fight in the dog," he must have had a terrier in mind.

A Family Tree Divide

Looking at the breeds in this group, it's not difficult to see that there are two main subgroups: "classic" working terriers—often wire-coated, less than knee high, intense, intelligent, agile, and independent hunters—and terriers who equally owe bulldogs for their genetics. This second group came about when breeders sought to take already feisty, high-energy terriers and beef them up—adding some of the notorious heft, brute strength, and stubbornness of bulldogs. Why create bull-and-terrier mixes in the first place? Nobody likes this answer, but for a long time the primary objective was fine-tuning the strong, fearless fighting dogs who would come to be known as pit bulls.

This wasn't a new idea—dogs had been bred to participate in blood "sports" for centuries. From at least the 1200s until the early 1800s, they had starring roles in the brutal spectacles of bullbaiting and bearbaiting. In 1835, however, things started to change. The gladiator-style fights were outlawed. It should have been the end of it, but it didn't take long for some of the folks who had made money in bullbaiting to shift their focus to an equally illegal but less conspicuous alternative: dogfights. You can find records of dogfights going back a thousand years (at least as far as ancient Molossus hounds versus English mastiffs), but this is the time when small-scale dogfights became a major form of entertainment and some greedy breeders put their all into creating ultimate fighting dogs.

I don't like to talk about this any more than people like to hear it, but there's no way to tell the story of the bull-terrier mixes—dogs who are often painted with one brush even though they are a number of different breeds and mixed breeds—without acknowledging this part of their history. The thing is, for most dogs, it's just that—one piece of their past. It should be one that's ancient history—just like the bulldog's history of bullbaiting and the mastiff's era as a war dog. But because the despicable practice of dogfighting is still going on today (despite being illegal almost everywhere in the world) and influencing some bloodlines, we have to acknowledge this small but dark corner in the terrier family. It's always important to really know your individual animal, to pay attention to more variables than breeding alone, and that's doubly important when we talk about the dog breeds that collectively get lumped under the pit bull umbrella.

So where do I stand on these dogs? I love working with them, because among all the shelter animals in the country, they're the ones who are least likely to get second chances. I pretty much almost always root for the underdog, and I love a good redemption story, and these dogs have tremendous potential to exemplify both.

Among individuals, there are *millions* of bull-influenced terriers and related mixed-breed dogs whose ancestors haven't seen an organized fight in at least a century. But due to reputations based on a small number of incidents, the breed type continues to be looked at as fighters more than lovers, and we're taught to fear them. I don't want any breed type written off as devils—or mistaken for angels, either. There's no such thing. There are simply dogs, each a combination of its genetics, age, sex, socialization, training, and the environment it lives in.

On the subject of genetics, bull-terrier mixes have been among the most heavily manipulated dogs, for better and for worse. During the height of the fighting-as-entertainment era, breeders strove to replicate their toughest, most intimidating and aggressive dogs—casting off the gentler and more timid pups. The fighters were the dogs that fueled fears that persist to this day—brutal and encouraged to violence against other dogs. In the intervening years, however, countless breeders have gone the other way—carrying on the bloodlines of the sweetest dogs from each litter and spaying/neutering the ones with aggression issues. The result of this tug-of-war between two different kinds of dogs is a lot of inconsistency, and so you need to understand and work with your individual dog and its temperament. Honestly, this is good advice no matter what breed your dog is. I've encountered aggressive dogs of almost every breed, and the most important factor in making sure they're not a danger is owners who are in control and who know their dog's triggers and warning signs.

Yes, some of these dogs can be a lot to handle, especially because they can be burly giants compared with classic terriers. But almost every terrier does best with an experienced, confident owner, and the bulldog-influenced breeds are no exception. Working with these dogs, testing their temperaments, understanding what makes them tick, and seeing them go on to be well-adjusted, loving pets is part of my calling.

Key Characteristics

Prey Drive in Overdrive

A lot of dog breeds are outstanding hunters—including dogs who track, tree, sight, scent, and retrieve. Most of these dogs, though, instinctively do their part of the job but don't go in for the kill (unless they're given a command to do so). Not so with terriers. They've been fine-tuned over centuries to see their work through, and the instinct for crittering—chasing and killing small animals—is in their blood.

Attitude

Being "game" is the most uniquely defining temperament characteristic for the terrier group. It means having a fighting spirit, and most of these dogs embody it from their head to their toes. Despite their (mostly) small size, they're eager to chase, unafraid of a fight, and totally confident. Old-time terrier breeders and owners took their respect for this quality to great lengths, even going so far as to devise tests for it involving live prey and minimum periods of "engagement." In other words, any terrier not actively looking for a fight wouldn't make the cut.

Intensity

A terrier is harder to tire out than a kid who's had two Cokes and a candy bar. I have a friend who likes to say that if you could take a Malinois and compact it down to fifteen pounds, you'd get a Jack Russell. These are big dogs compressed into tiny bodies, and they carry themselves with great intensity. Most terriers are not quiet little dogs who'll want to sit in your lap. They want *action*. They want to *do stuff.*

Stubbornness

Okay, terriers aren't actually stubborn, because that's a human characteristic. But they're confident and they're intelligent, and that combination sometimes finds them focused on things other than training. For the same reasons, sometimes there's a disconnect between a terrier knowing the rules and choosing to follow them. I have a Scottish friend who refers to her misbehaving terrier as a "cheeky little bugger." She doesn't love him any less for it. Honestly, I think she loves him a little more.

Athleticism

Physically, the most common characteristic in earth dogs is their small size. There are outlier breeds, including the Airedale and some of the bull-terrier mixes, but for the working terriers of the past, being any bigger than the rat, fox, or badger they needed to pursue into its den was a deal breaker. A big dog just can't "go to ground" in a small hole.

Regardless of their size, though, terriers are typically fast and agile—even acrobatic. I've taught terriers to dance, to jump into a handler's arms, to leap over obstacles, and to do all kinds of tricks and agility challenges. Once they've gotten into the groove of training, these dogs love doing the work. They respond well to physical and mental challenges, and learning to do something new and executing it for a reward is an impulse they embrace.

Heart

If the overall description of terriers makes them sound a little like small furry four-legged terrorists, let's put that in perspective. Yes, these dogs are a handful, but for the most part, they're trouble in the same way Dennis the Menace and Pippi Longstocking are trouble—naughty, rebellious, sometimes misguided, totally lovable. They're complex and intelligent, sometimes assertive, and they make us laugh out loud. Over the years I've rescued more terriers and terrier mixes than I can count, many of them who have come from terribly neglectful and abusive circumstances. This is often because of that disconnect between appearance and behavior I mentioned—people want a cute little dog, and when they discover the one in their lives is willful and energetic and the opposite of compliant, they're far too quick to throw in the towel. But even the terriers who have been treated poorly and abandoned amaze me time and again with their capacity to become loving and playful again.

Trainability

Terriers require an investment of time and energy to build trust and understanding before they'll be willing to learn from you. Because of this, far too many of them are surrendered by owners who give up and say they're "impossible" or "untrainable." I urge you to be persistent, though, because when you break through with most terriers, when you reach the point where you connect and they start learning, there's almost nothing they can't be taught. If you invest the time in connecting, motivating, and training these dogs, they can truly be like learning machines. They are worth your effort.

Behavior Challenges and Possible Solutions

Drive

Prey drive is more than just a common trait, it's also the root of many terriers' behavior challenges. Think about it: it's a defining characteristic that these dogs have the kind of drive you'd expect to see in a starving wolf—no matter how cute they are on the outside or how sweet they might be when there's nothing around to hunt. Now that we have actual exterminators who manage intrusive wildlife, the terrier who's always looking to do the job comes up empty. Like an oar on a speedboat, he's purpose-built for a job that doesn't need doing. The result can be restlessness, a sense of searching, and frustration—and that's where the problems begin.

The solution here isn't rocket science. Figure out a way to let your terrier fulfill his destiny. It doesn't have to involve blood and guts. Experiment with toys that engage your dog and play with them in ways that pique and satisfy his prey drive. Fetch (with multiple balls if your terrier doesn't actually retrieve), Frisbee, blowing bubbles for him to pop, and even running remote-controlled toys (with close supervision) all give you opportunities to engage your dog's prey drive in safe, acceptable ways.

Aggressiveness

The hard-to-quantify personality trait of big attitude runs deep in most terriers—so much so that owners need to be sure that it doesn't go too far and turn into aberrational behaviors like fighting with other dogs or being aggressive with strangers. Also remember that terriers are often afflicted with Napoléon syndrome—they may not give a second thought to provoking or even aggressively engaging a much bigger dog. The first step to managing this attitude is simple: never allow or encourage negative enjoyment of it, and never reward your dog for looking for a fight. Just because your dog wakes up every morning ready to take on the world doesn't mean you should let her.

Second, give her a healthy outlet for all that energy. Go for a run, play keep-away in the yard, wrestle with a tug toy. In a dog for whom this trait is managed, it's just another piece of a big, engaging personality.

Third, figure out where your dog's personal "bubble" begins and ends and learn to recognize any body language that leads up to aggressive or defensive behavior. The overwhelming majority of dogs use body language and/or vocalization to show when they're annoyed well before they go for a bite or tackle. As an owner, it's part of your job to know the difference, for example, between the friendly wag of a tail and one that's a warning flag.

Bossiness

If your terrier could talk, there's little doubt that some of his barking rants would roughly translate to "You're not the boss of me" or "My house, my rules." It's like there's a wee curmudgeon inside some of these dogs, one who defaults to the assumption that he or she is in a position of authority. You can gently and consistently remind your terrier that there's already an alpha in the family by routinely expecting simple obedience responses before meals and treats. This isn't about you being a drill sergeant; it's about incorporating obedience just like exercise, play, and affection into your dog's routine.

Grooming is another opportunity to bond with your dog and very gently reinforce the idea that there's no leadership void in your home. Being brushed is a simple, pleasurable experience for most dogs, one that helps them feel secure and connected to you. Since many terriers have high-maintenance coats, you can think of the time you spend grooming as doing double duty.

Scrappy Nature

Terriers, more than many other breed groups, like to be in charge. They like to feel confident that they're the "big dog" in any given space. The presence of another dog can call that into question, and rather than taking a *more the merrier* attitude, they may instead go with one that's more *king of the hill*. The form this takes can range from something as harmless as adopting imperious body language (or climbing on furniture to gain a height advantage) to outright confrontation.

The best way to deal with this common behavior issue is a combination of early socialization with plenty of other dogs in varied situations, and a strong obedience foundation (so your dog accepts that a NO from you is the last word). You can't whisk your dog back to puppyhood to accomplish the first of these advantages, but it's never too late to start obedience training. You may not be able to change the way your terrier feels about other dogs, but you can certainly teach her to sit quietly and tolerate their presence when you ask.

Training Resistance

Almost all terriers can be trained, and once they get on board they're great at it. But getting their engagement can be a unique challenge. They don't default to innate cooperation like some breeds (looking at you, retrievers). You've got to convince them. The trick in most cases comes down to making it interesting and fun for the dog. Terriers like to play, to run, to think, to be both silly and smart. Make training a game, mix up your use of different treats and play rewards, and keep sessions short (but do them often).

One key thing I've found in training terriers is that they respond extremely well to play rewards—often better than they do to food rewards. Personally I like to mix up both, using food rewards during a session and a play reward at the end. For these dogs, it's the kind of play that matters. Choose a toy your dog is likely to love (my own terriers loved anything with a bushy texture—toys that looked and felt like squirrels' tails, basically). Don't just give your dog that toy. Instead, build up its aura. Take it out and send it zooming by, then put it away (you can literally zoom it if you put it on a string). This will pique your dog's interest. Repeat a few times, making sure your terrier is fully fixed on the toy. At the end of your next short, successful training session, pull out that toy and let your dog have it—just for a few minutes. She'll quickly figure out that the toy is a reward for a job well done.

Barking

Terriers tend to bark a lot. It's a part of who they are and not something that's going to be fully eradicated. Rather than trying to train your dog not to bark (a losing proposition), work on the NO command to teach your dog to *stop* barking. Using a handful of pennies in a plastic bottle or a Shake & Break training tool will help in this process as you interrupt your dog's barking, then give him a treat for being quiet.

Digging

Digging is in terriers' blood. It was part of the way they earned their keep for centuries, and many of them tackle it with joy and dedication. In a way, digging is their art—the thing they do to create something original and uniquely theirs in the world. Now I know you don't want your yard to look like a minefield, but I'm guessing we can all agree that terriers need every outlet for energy and creativity they can get. With that in mind, I'm a fan of redirecting digging rather than trying to stop it entirely. Instead of constantly fighting this, designate a Dig Here area and encourage your dog to use that spot. Make it interesting. Bury toys. Digging is both a physical and a mental outlet, so if at all possible for *you*, make it possible for your dog.

Door Dashing

The typical terrier is afflicted with a serious case of FOMA (Fear Of Missing Anything). That desire to be busy and involved in every little thing frequently translates to door dashing and running away. Small size, great speed, and athleticism all contribute to terriers' success in these endeavors, squeezing themselves under, through, and around your legs the minute the door cracks open. And if your dog perceives any kind of prey on the other side of the door or fence, you can expect him to show absolutely no loyalty to anything but the chase.

Given how much time terrier owners can end up spending chasing after and bringing home their dogs, it's well worth investing a few hours and some energy into teaching your dog not to bolt through every open door.

The #1 Command

Like the hounds, terriers' extreme prey drive means that when something catches their attention, it can be a struggle for you to get it back. When that happens, your dog becomes an instant flight risk. You can help keep your dog safe and close to home by teaching a reliable recall command. When you train and practice this one, consider also training with a whistle. The reason for this is that a more distinctive sound will cut through any "noise"—not just the ambient sound wherever your dog happens to be, but also the clamoring demand to chase he's sensing in his head. Practice with a long line, without and then with distractions. If you put in the time, your dog will respond to your command or the whistle on autopilot. Teaching this command will give you peace of mind in all kinds of situations, including door-dashing moments, dog park adventures, and escapes from the yard.

Great Examples

American Staffordshire Terrier

Deep among the hallowed lanes of Gettysburg National Military Park, the monument erected for the Eleventh Pennsylvania Infantry unit looks at first glance like many of the others commemorating soldiers who fought and died during its historic Civil War battle. A bronze soldier stands weary but battle-ready on a granite pedestal, his musket and bayonet raised in the air. But at the bottom of the memorial, a different hero gets her due—a dog named Sallie, the only dog represented on the field who actually went to war. Her statue is stocky and muscular, with a broad, square head; high, folded ears; and a shortened snout. She's lying on her belly and looking up—her eyes weary but devoted. It's a tribute to a uniquely treasured American Staffordshire terrier, or "AmStaff."

Legend has it Sallie was delivered to the regimental commander in a basket when she was just a puppy. Whether or not that's true, records show that she was much more than a mascot. She was the beloved and personal pet of the men in her unit. She went to Chancellorsville, Antietam, and Bull Run beside the regiment, and at Gettysburg she stood guard over her wounded and dead comrades. Nearly two years later when she was shot and killed on yet another battlefield, several soldiers stopped to bury their dog, even in the midst of heavy gunfire. It would be another twenty-four years before the monument was constructed, but even then, decades after they knew her, the regiment's survivors voted unanimously to include Sallie's likeness.

I include her here because Sallie's story is about her devotion and the strength of the bonds she formed, and those are traits that too often get overlooked when we talk about this breed and all the similar and mixed-breed dogs that get lumped in with it. The fact is, every day bully-type dogs serve as loyal companions, patient therapy dogs, and treasured family pets.

The history of AmStaffs in the US goes back to the mid-1800s, when Staffordshire terriers arrived from Britain. Of course *bigger is better* is the American way, and this applied directly to the development of the AmStaff—dogs that are typically several inches taller and as much as twice the weight of their British cousins. Their size just adds to their athleticism, and these are dogs that are happiest and healthiest when they're getting sixty to ninety minutes of vigorous exercise every day. They're great jogging partners, fun companions in the yard and on hikes, and they're snuggly at the end of the day. I've met quite a few of these dogs who are so intent on cuddling they can be a little clingy—they don't seem to realize they are far too big to be lap-dogs. Sweet as they can be, however, AmStaffs are a lot of dog, and for that reason they do best with experienced owners who are comfortable and confident in the alpha role of their household pack.

Fox Terrier

The fox terrier was once considered very much a "gentleman's dog," and the British gentry loved their horses and their hunts. This breed's highly specialized work was in a different vein than that of the fox *hounds*, who would run out ahead to sniff out prey and corner it. While the hounds were beating feet, you could find the terriers perched comfortably alongside their owners—in their saddlebags.

Designed to go underground after their prey, fox terriers were turned loose when the hounds had done the cornering. At that point, the feisty terriers would dive fearlessly into the den. A good terrier left its prey with just two outcomes from which to choose: run back out of the hole to face the waiting hounds and hunters, or get dragged out by the throat. It was a catch-22 scenario—one that almost never ended well for the fox.

Fox terriers come in two varieties—smooth and wire. They're highly similar except for their coat (the wire variety has that distinctive beard). In either form, these are the Energizer bunnies of dogs—always in motion, busy, and curious. Even though they're born hunters, they're also very much indoor family dogs.

Jack Russell Terrier

Without the fox terrier, there would be no Jack Russell. Dogs like Pepe were bred to hunt rodents and foxes, and unlike many of our modern breeds, not only can their breed history be traced back to a specific point, but we can follow it to a particular person and the logic he used in the process. That man was Reverend John Russell in Devonshire, England, and his objective was to build a better fox hunter.

Russell wrote a letter explaining his process, saying he had started with a smooth terrier—the baseline of fox-hunting dogs. He bred this dog with an Italian greyhound, seeking puppies who would be sleeker and faster than a terrier alone—but still small. Apparently the ears on these pups weren't acceptable to Russell (he called them an "eyesore"), so the next generation added beagle to the mix. Finally, to the growing recipe for the perfect terrier, Russell engaged a bulldog to "give the necessary courage." The resulting dogs, which Russell continued to fine-tune, were in many ways ultimate terriers—fast, fearless, agile to the point of being acrobatic, and extremely smart. They were also mostly white, which was a key feature in fox hunting as it made them instantly distinguishable from the foxes themselves if and when both creatures came tumbling out of a den.

These dogs would also become one of the most energetic breeds in an already frenetic group. A typical Jack is in fifth gear from dawn to dusk—he doesn't know any other way to be.

I've had two of these dogs myself and can attest to the fact that they don't limit themselves to fox hunting. They are incredibly efficient ratters. I lost count of how many rats my own dogs wiped out, and until they brought it to my attention I didn't even know I *had* rats. It's important for any terrier owner, and especially any owner of a JRT, to know the instinct to do the work in these dogs is still strong, unbendable even. For this reason and to avoid the kind of boredom they're prone to (the kind that is either mischievous or destructive), they need to be engaged and challenged and exercised to exhaustion every single day. Don't let their adorable exteriors fool you, because these are truly high-performance dogs.

Technically, at this writing, the American Kennel Club doesn't recognize the Jack Russell, but does register both Russell and Parson terriers. Unless you're an expert on show dogs, there's a good chance you would find those two breeds indistinguishable—and likely call them both Jack Russells on sight. I think most dogs would not take any offense. It's great to be a JRT by any name. Despite the fact that they can be a handful to manage and train, their colorful, entertaining, feisty personalities inspire love and loyalty.

More Terriers

Airedale. The so-called King of Terriers is the biggest of the classic working terriers, and it's also an intelligent, versatile all-around dog. These dogs were bred by crossing small regional terriers with otterhounds—with a goal of creating energetic working dogs who could double as guard dogs, work in the water as needed, and hold their own against outsize prey like raccoons, foxes, and badgers. The breed evolved into an ideal farm dog that could truly do a little bit of everything—hunting (not just vermin but also big game), guarding, and herding.

Airedales' adaptability also earned them work as police and military dogs. They played a historic role in World War I, when thousands of them went to battle alongside British Isle forces. Just like on the farms they came from, the dogs were multitalented, but they specialized in carrying communications between encampments. Their persistent, never-quit attitudes meant they would see their jobs through—including in documented cases where the dogs pushed on to their destinations after being gravely wounded along the way.

Airedales are big dogs in more ways than one. Like their bodies, their personalities are outsize. They're highly energetic, confident, and intelligent—a combination that can appear as stubbornness and defiance and can pose significant training challenges. It is absolutely worth seeing that training through with these dogs, though, because once they learn and accept the rules, they're loving, loyal, intuitive pets.

Bedlington Terrier. The Bedlington's pedigree can be traced back, unbroken, to 1782, the year before the British formally recognized American independence, making it the terrier with the longest known line. Originally bred in an English mining town, these dogs may look like little lambs, but their personalities are profoundly influenced by their wolf origins as well as their unique combination of canine genetics. These little dogs were developed by crossing whippets and terriers. The whippet DNA made them lightning fast, and they were among the best crittering dogs as a result. As workers, they were determined, fierce hunters who could kill rats and mice at home or in the mine. They could even chase a badger into its den and emerge victorious.

Despite their hard-charging origins, most Bedlingtons have made the shift to the role of household pets pretty gracefully. They shed very little and are sociable and loving, two of the most in-demand criteria for family pets. They're smart enough to distinguish between guests and intruders. Even though these are very much true terriers who can be barky and bossy, they tend to be a little mellower than some of their cousin breeds. As long as Bedlingtons get sufficient exercise and mental stimulation, they can be well-behaved indoor dogs and great companions.

Border Terrier. These dogs are sometimes seen as the country cousins of the terrier world. While plenty of terriers were bred for specific looks, in many ways this breed is the dogs who were left over—they are typically a medium brown, and they look perpetually scruffy and scrappy (in the cutest possible way). The thing is, sometimes not being the apple of the breeder's eye has its rewards, and that's the case with border terriers, who have consistently cheerful, attentive personalities and overall good health.

The breed gets its name from the area where it originated—the border between England and Scotland. Even though they're small dogs (typically around fifteen inches tall and fifteen pounds), they're tough. They've historically done double duty, guarding sheep in addition to serving as small-prey hunters.

Bull Terrier. The bull terrier may have the most distinctive head in the dog world. Shaped like a football, or an egg, that long, bony oval with small eyes and pointy ears makes this breed almost instantly recognizable—and every once in a while gets him confused with a piglet. In keeping with their funny faces, these dogs tend to have silly, playful personalities. They're generally confident, cheerful, and eager to be part of the family.

True to the bulldog part of their roots, bull terriers can be headstrong; true to their classic terrier origins, they can be assertive. They do best with calm, consistent leadership combined with plenty of opportunities both to exercise and to play.

Cairn Terrier. Terriers are diggers by nature, never afraid to get their feet dirty and relishing excavation opportunities. The centuries-old breed can be traced back to the Scottish Isle of Skye, but when these hardworking ratters finally made their way to "the show"—when owners tried to register the breed—the name Skye terrier was taken by their bat-eared, long-haired cousins. Cairns ended up with a more humble name—one that translates to "rock" terrier.

Small, sturdy, cheerful, and boisterous, cairns are loving pets. Like so many of their terrier cousins, there is nothing that makes them happier than the opportunity to spend time outside exploring, off leash if possible. One of the most famous and beloved movie-star dogs of all time—Toto from *The Wizard of Oz*—was a cairn.

Dandie Dinmont. This is a rare breed, but one with far too rich a backstory to leave out. Scottish farmer James Davidson didn't create these terriers, but he did specialize in them, and his dogs caught the eye of Walter Scott, one of the most prolific novelists and poets of the early 1800s. Both the dogs and the farmer must have made a big impression on Scott, because his 1815 release *Guy Mannering* featured not just the jaunty light-colored terriers with the huge eyes, short legs, long spines, and the canine version of a pompadour but also their owner—a guy he named Dandie Dinmont. The name got tied up with the image of the dogs, and for the next decade they were a fad all over Europe. *Guy Mannering* did for Dandies in their time what Lassie would later do for collies and *Call of the Wild* for St. Bernard–shepherd mixes—it put them on every family's radar.

Irish Terrier. Known for its distinctive reddish coat, the Irish terrier has been a beloved farm dog in Ireland for generations. Unlike many of their terrier cousins, which earned their keep almost exclusively going after rodents and small game, these dogs have a wider historical résumé. They've been all-around and versatile farm dogs and companions.

Even though very few of them still work on farms, the breed continues to be a popular, energetic, and affectionate pet.

Miniature Schnauzer. Here's a breed that strayed pretty far from its original purpose as it shrunk in size. Standard schnauzers were first developed in Germany as all-around farm dogs. They could guard, herd, hunt—and kill rodents in their spare time. What they could not do was dive down into a subterranean den and drive their quarry out or dispatch it in the hole. And so the light bulb moment . . . *If only these great multitasking dogs were smaller* . . . occurred, and over generations the German schnauzers were shrunk by breeding until they were the perfect size to go to ground and catch rats, mice, and other vermin. (Someone also had a light bulb moment in wondering about bigger dogs, which led to the development of the giant schnauzer.)

Small and confident, with a distinctive heavy brow line, miniature schnauzers tend to be very vocal, wanting to keep you informed about everything going on outside the windows and doors. They're fun, playful, and affectionate, but like many terriers, they don't give their hearts to just anyone. They're independent, and you have to earn your way in. Once you do, though, they're loyal and loving compadres for life.

Norfolk and Norwich Terriers. Even among other terrier breeds, these two are small fry—among the littlest terriers. They look almost alike, distinguishable mostly by their ears (Norwich ears are pointy and upright; Norfolk ears are folded). Both breeds have such sweet faces and wiry coats it's easy to assume they're simply lovey lapdogs, but don't let the cuteness fool you. These dogs have a long hunting history, and while they may not be a match for a badger or a fox, they can dispatch mice and rats all day long.

Both the Norwich and the Norfolk were bred to hunt and work in packs rather than as individuals, and their resulting sociability is probably why they're typically quick to bond with people and with other family pets. They've got enough affection and personality to spread around. These are dogs who will make you laugh one day and make you want to tear your hair out the next. To keep the hair pulling to a minimum, give them lots of exercise. A lot of people adopt these dogs and mixed breeds with their characteristics in pairs, because two friends will help tire each other out and take some of that responsibility off the family.

Rat Terrier. Though its historical origins hark back to Britain's fox terriers, the rat terrier breed is as American as apple pie. In the early and mid-1900s these dogs were ubiquitous on small farms and rural homesteads. They were also in the White House, where it's rumored Teddy Roosevelt gave them their name because of their very specific talent. A crew of terriers in New York, including one of these distinctive pups, goes out nights to help the city manage its rat problem. It's remarkable to see not just how efficiently a terrier team can dispatch rodents on their own but also how they know to work together to find their prey, get them out in the open, and block them from running away. They are truly consummate hunters.

Also, if you need a dog that's a 100 percent nonshedder, look no further than the southern cousin of the rat terrier. When a Louisiana breeder happened to discover a hairless pup in a new litter, that dog was the beginning of an offshoot breed, the rare American hairless terrier.

Scottish Terrier. For more than seventy years, kids around the world have been calling dibs on one of two iconic game pieces inside every Monopoly box. They want to be the race car or they want to be the dog—a pert-looking Scottie who looks ready to run the bases. The iron or the pocketbook? Not a chance. The Scottie's looks are iconic and distinctive: their solidly boxy little bodies, their alert ears, the long wispy eyebrows that give them that permanently disapproving expression. Inside every Scottie there's a spirited old man who carries himself with dignity and confidence, one who can be by turns endearing and disapproving. This is a dog with attitude, but one that is always fun.

As popular pets, Scotties (along with Westies) are among the breeds that have been ever-so-slightly mellowed from their terrier ways with time. They're still rambunctious and need thirty to sixty minutes of exercise every day, but they do have some low gears.

Staffordshire Bull Terrier. The smaller, older British cousins of American Staffordshires, these dogs are low, square, and solid—as sturdy as a dog can be. Despite their fighting dog origins, they tend to be extremely lovey-dovey with their people and can be beloved family pets. It's impossible for me to look at these dogs and not feel frustration at their past. They were bred to fight and forced to fight, and now they continue to have to carry that legacy both in their genes and in their reputations. It's a disservice to a breed that is otherwise cheerful and devoted.

Like the other hefty terriers, Staffies can be hard to handle on leash and require a great deal of vigorous exercise. Teach them the HEEL command while they're young and practice often. The more obedience fundamentals you can teach your dog, the better an ambassador she'll be for her breed and the more secure she'll be as a pet. Some Staffordshire terriers and mixes do fine with other pets, but others are intolerant of cats and other dogs. It's not uncommon for this breed to be happiest and healthiest in a one-dog home.

West Highland Terrier. There are a few terriers for whom hunting is farther back in their collective history than others, and this breed is one of them. Westies have been bred primarily as pets for decades, and it shows in their somewhat curbed prey drive and their ability to relax, even nap once in a while. Don't let their cuteness mislead you, though. These sturdy little dogs are still high energy and they have minds of their own—and they're often big barkers. Like all terriers, a Westie will need to choose you before it'll be affectionate, but they are otherwise sweet-natured, good with kids, and easy to train with a little patience and persistence.

Wheaten Terrier. The soft-coated Wheaten is not named for a place or a person or a job like most of the terrier breeds. Instead, the name is a tribute to their shiny flowing coats. This breed also hails from Ireland, where it served as a versatile farm dog. Despite its working outdoor origins, Wheatens tend to love their creature comforts. This is a dog who'll want to be on the sofa and in the bed, who'll hog your pillow and burrow under your blankets. They love kids and love to play. Like almost all terriers, they're also willful. They respond best to positive training and rewards. If you're harsh with one of these dogs, you're likely to get an earful back from him.

Conclusion

The terriers are a group known for their high energy, high prey drive, and big personalities. They are feisty (in fact, the origin of the word goes back to an early group of terriers called *feists*). Terriers are not necessarily sociable with other dogs, but they can be great family pets. They are very trainable despite their sometimes-stubborn intelligence, and they should be trained, because if you don't establish some order in their lives, they'll soon rule the world.

IDEAL COMPANIONS AT HOME AND IN THE FIELD: THE SPORTING GROUP

Of all the breed groups, the sporting dogs are typically the most eager to please and among the most trainable (and it's no coincidence those two things go together). They earn their long-standing reputation for being loyal, loving, and (mostly) well-mannered family pets every day.

I don't have to look any further to see that than my own backyard, where my flat-coated retriever, Koda, is my pal, security chief, and canine right-hand man when it comes to working with the dogs who come and go in our pack. Some are visiting, some are training, and some are waiting for forever homes—but they all have to learn to be part of the family and get along while they're here.

Koda was just nine months old when I brought him home to begin training as a service dog. I believed he had what it takes to do this noble work, and I was looking forward to getting him in shape for the job. Even though he was a big dog in what we call an "awkward stage" when we talk about teenagers, and even though he still had a lot of puppy in him, he passed the early phases with flying colors. He was smart and attentive, picking up his 7 Common Commands like he was born to them, impressing me day after day.

But then we hit a snag the first (and second, and third) time Koda broke training to take off after a squirrel.

Look, retrievers have prey drive, but if there were a sliding scale of it among dog breeds, they'd be on the low end. A Jack Russell like my dog Pepe would be all the way to the right—a red-hot level ten with a manic commitment that can basically only be interrupted if you can catch and tackle the dog. But most retrievers come in somewhere around a two or three on that same scale. A lot of them just watch squirrels and other small animals with passing interest, maybe thumping their tails a little. Some get riled up enough to pursue, but usually not for long—just a burst of speed and the moment's over. Generally speaking, it's not hard to see that what's an obsession for hounds and terriers is more of an amusement for more sporting dogs.

With that in mind, I figured I could teach Koda to comply when I called him off.

Six months later, after working with this dog day in and day out, I realized I was wrong. Koda was extremely well trained, and he had a steady disposition, but he was like a junkie when it came to going after prey-size animals—he just couldn't lay off. At a mature weight of about eighty pounds, not only was he still incorrigibly lumbering after squirrels, he was also leaving the occasional dead mouse or rat on my doorstep.

The consequences of putting a dog with out-of-control prey drive into service were too serious to risk. He could take off and get lost. He could leave his handler in a moment when he or she really needed help. He could inadvertently cause an injury. With all that in mind, I knew I had to flunk him and start over with another dog.

The bright side is that very few animals are as terrific at being pets as failed service dogs. Koda was keen and attentive; he knew not just the basic commands but some next-level ones as well; he was playful and gentle at the right times. I had a long list of people hoping to adopt from the ranch, so one day I start making inquiries into who would be the best match. The next morning started with a light bulb moment: I'd spent the better part of a year working this dog, giving him patience and guidance. He'd given me gray hairs, laughs, and regrets about not being able to put him on the job. He had learned *everything* I'd ever asked him to learn—except for the ability to resist a chase.

Was I going to send Koda away? Couldn't do it. I was annoyed with this prey-crazy retriever, but I was also deeply attached. Plus, he owed me. One way or another I wanted to put this dog to work.

At first, just-a-pet Koda was a ridiculously oversize ratter and an imposing presence when strangers came to my door. It wasn't long, though, before he moved into another, more valuable role. He became the leader of the ever-changing pack at the ranch, and he was great at it—knowing when to be mild and when to be tough, when to give a new dog some space and when to get close, and how to shut down spats between dogs in the yard with little more than a look or a grunt. He knew how to provide comfort or correction—whatever the moment needed. And he constantly led by example. More and more I found myself standing back and letting him handle small moments when trouble was brewing. Koda doesn't even have to fight to make peace—he's that good. He exudes calm and authority, occasionally body blocks a dog who needs a time-out, and everybody in the yard learns from and respects him.

Do you know how much more effective it is for a strong, benevolent dog to teach another dog than it is for a human to do it? They've been raising puppies and living in packs and taking care of their own for thousands of years, since they were wolves. Within their own circle, it happens naturally.

Koda's a credit to sporting dogs everywhere, exercising the level temperament, gentle nature, and good judgment of a retriever. He's long since paid off his training debt in helping me manage the pack. The days of me looking at this guy and seeing a failure are long gone, because he's an indispensable part of my team and my family. In an entirely different way from what I expected, he did end up doing noble work, helping me rehabilitate dogs and place them in forever homes. He makes my job much easier. He's a whole different kind of service dog.

The Hunters' Helper

Sporting dogs go by a lot of monikers besides their breed names. People call them bird dogs, gun dogs, upland or lowland hunters, wetland hunters, and just generically retrievers, pointers, setters, and spaniels. The variety of ways we categorize them is a hint at how many unique hunting challenges breeders were looking to address with this group—and just how specialized some of them are. Overall, though, the most remarkable thing about the sporting dogs may be that as a group their instincts to hunt became fully entwined with the desire to help their handlers. The result? Dogs who will hunt for a person before they'll hunt for themselves. You can find pointers, setters, spaniels, and retrievers with a wide range of innate drives, and equally with instincts that cause them to keep one eye on their human—to try to maintain that connection.

Without training to hone their hunting skills so they hold a point or wait for the hunter's signal to run ahead or to retrieve, these urges can look like a jumble of pointless impulses. Your Labrador retriever, Irish setter, or Brittany may freeze at the sight of a bird, may not be able to take its eyes off it, may charge at any flying object (tennis ball, anyone?), may pick up every stick in the park and drop them all at your feet. A hundred years ago all those deeply held instincts would have been honed and polished, practiced and rewarded, until the sporting dog could perform in the field with little more than an occasional hand signal or whistle for direction.

Today, among the dogs who don't get this training (though many of them still do), we've discovered that sporting breeds' particular skill sets, and their unique temperaments, can transfer almost seamlessly to family life. Yes, they need exercise (a *lot* of it). Yes, sometimes they do silly doggie things and have to be corrected. They chew and they jump. They shed. And yes, there is a small minority among them who have serious behavior issues like aggression or seemingly incurable separation anxiety.

But those are the few. The many are the dogs that hike mountains by our sides, romp with the kids in the yard, warn us of approaching strangers but warmly greet friends, and sleep quietly at the foot of the bed at night. These are dogs who are, thanks to their breed histories, well and naturally suited to being pets. It's no fluke that retrievers are commonly America's most popular dogs for decades now.

Three Main Jobs

Historically, sporting dogs fulfill at least one of three roles to earn their keep, as pointers/setters, spaniels, or retrievers:

Pointers/Setters. These dogs are a sophisticated detection system unto themselves. Long before binoculars, drones, thermal imaging, and hidden woodland cameras, there were dogs capable of moving quietly at a hunter's side, tuned in to every scent and sound in the marsh or forest. Their job required attention and restraint—discovering the location of prey (usually birds) and using age-old body language to communicate that information. Setters were long favored by hunters using nets, because they crouch down low as they indicate the presence of prey. Pointers are ideally suited to firearm hunters, as they stand and orient themselves toward their prey.

Spaniels. The spaniel's primary job is to flush out prey (again, usually birds) so that the hunter can dispatch it. At first consideration, it seems like any dog could run in and scare birds into the air, but this job is done in close and typically silent cooperation with the hunter. It requires the dog to know where the birds are, to be watching for a signal (often a hand signal), and to move on the hunter's mark.

Retrievers. The retriever is the one who brings home the bacon (or in this case, the duck or the pheasant). After shots are fired, these are the dogs sent to locate and ever-so-gently bring the birds back to the hunter. This job can be much harder and more complex than it sounds, as lowland hunting often requires the dog to wade, slog, or swim through swamps and ponds at all temperatures, and it demands they return the birds in the same condition they find them. A dog who mangles a duck in transit isn't doing the hunter any favors. Ask anybody who's tried to do this kind of hunting with a nonretriever, and you're likely to hear tales of dogs who demolished or even ate the birds en route to their handlers. This is what makes the retrievers so unique to the rest of the sporting group—a naturally soft grip that's perfect for the job.

In practice, these sporting jobs don't always need to be done by different dogs. The breeds in this group largely got their names based on the job in which they specialized, but hunters— past and present—don't need to work with one of each of these animals in tow. It's not an assembly line. Some hunt with one or two specialists, and many capitalize on their sporting dog's natural ability—and also teach it to do at least one of the other jobs. There are some breeds, especially the continental European breeds (versus the British ones) that were deliberately bred for an ability to multitask. Dogs like the German shorthaired pointer, the vizsla, and the Weimaraner are all versatile workers by design, and are sometimes called HPR dogs (short for hunt, point, retrieve).

Distinctions Within Breeds

In many dog breeds, there are subgroups that are considerably different from one another. One of the big ways this happens is when dogs are bred for separate purposes. In the Lab, the most popular dogs in the US, it's especially pronounced. There are breeders who have been focused on creating perfect hunting dogs for decades, and there are those striving to create ideal companion dogs and—with an even higher bar—service dogs. Hunting lines are typically high energy with strong prey drive. On the other end of the spectrum, service dog lines have lower energy and prey drive (at least the ones that are successful at it!). Whether you have a registered purebred dog, a rescue, or a Lab mix of unknown origin, your dog's family history may play a part in the kind of behavior you'll find yourself dealing with. You can sometimes tell these subgroups of dogs apart by their appearance—companion and service-bred dogs are stockier and less athletic than their tall, lean, and very eager hunting cousins.

At Your Service

A number of factors combine in the alchemy of a perfect service dog, and there's no breed group that exemplifies more of these than sporting dogs. In fact, most of the service dogs I've trained came from this group—especially Labs and golden retrievers. Let's take a look at why they're ideal candidates (keeping in mind that it is only the best of the best that get through service training):

1. Temperament. A service dog doesn't merely need to be calm and composed; it needs to be nearly bombproof. In many cases, these dogs are entrusted with some aspect of the safety of their owners, and so these are sacred partnerships. Dogs who are fearful, aggressive, easily spooked, or distracted need not apply. At their core, most sporting dogs are sweet and stable. This is absolutely critical. You can't know who or what might come along and shake up a service dog's expectations or routines, so you have to be able to count on the dog to be the reliable factor.

2. Size and Strength. Bigger than a breadbox; smaller than a pony . . . In all seriousness, there is an optimum size for service dogs whose work encompasses physical tasks. That size falls somewhere between being small enough to easily navigate any room or curl up at her handler's feet without being obtrusive—and big enough to be sturdy, strong, and in many cases, suitably stable to cooperate with a BRACE command. BRACE is something we teach many dogs who work with individuals who have limited mobility. Wearing a specially fitted harness that distributes weight, these dogs are able to allow their owners to lean on them to sit, stand, navigate stairs, and make transfers to and from wheelchairs. This is an invaluable service that gives handlers more freedom to move around without asking another person for help—a true tool of independence. As you might guess, dogs have to be a certain height to be able to perform this job. Thigh-to-hip height on the handler is ideal. The dogs also have to be physically sound. I'd never ask a dog to routinely do a job that could cause pain or injury, and the strong, sturdy build of sporting dogs makes them able to do this work with ease. The physics of the task are simply impossible for a dog that is too small (like a basset hound), too delicate (like a saluki), or built with a spine that can't handle pressure.

3. *Careful Retrieval.* I can teach almost any dog to go get an item and bring it back, but I cannot teach all of them to deliver it in one piece. The sporting breeds in general and retrievers in particular have been bred with a "soft mouth"—an incredibly gentle touch that allows them to pick up downed birds and deliver them undamaged to a hunter. In the service world, this means the dog can perform one of the most needed jobs—getting things and bringing them to the handler on command. From phones and remotes to keys and mail, the dog's ability to deliver makes life easier for her person. Sporting dogs are reliable and trustworthy with whatever you need them to get. My experience teaching most other breeds this skill has involved receiving stuff (*my* stuff) in pieces: mangled sunglasses, a remote with permanent tooth marks, even a phone with a cracked screen. Those dogs didn't know they were doing something wrong, of course. This, like Koda's squirrel problem, is a deal breaker. I can't give a service dog to someone with the caveat that he's going to handle retrieval jobs with all the finesse of a crocodile.

Key Characteristics

A Biddable Nature

Being biddable is the hallmark trait of most sporting dogs. In a nutshell, it means the dog is compliant—wanting to please and capable of responding well to training. In general, a sporting dog wants what you want. Sometimes you have to be creative or persistent to convey what it is you have in mind, but you should consistently have an attentive, well-intentioned partner in a pointer, setter, spaniel, or retriever. After centuries of breeding to make these dogs true partners to their owners, it is simply in their nature to want to work with you.

Trainability

The jobs that sporting breeds have long been bred to do require both constant cooperation with the handler and also the capacity for independent thought. These dogs are often bred and trained to be multitaskers, unlike some breeds that have been designed to focus solely and with great intensity on one thing (pick a hound, any hound). As a result, they've got great capacity to learn—not just what you deliberately teach them, but also what they observe on their own. These are dogs who will learn your schedule and become as good as a clock in anticipating it. They'll constantly expand their vocabularies until you find yourself running out of words to substitute for "walk" or "treat" to keep their excitement in check. They'll quickly learn their way around the neighborhood and will likely remember places you've taken them to visit in the past.

Friendliness

Some dogs are born reactionaries—poised to freak out at the slightest incursion of any strange person, animal, or object into their environment. Many will do this perpetually, going into five-alarm-fire mode day after day when the mail arrives, for example, or when a familiar neighbor walks past your door. In general, the sporting breeds show a lot more discretion. Many will become guarded at the sight of a stranger, but can recognize the appearance of the mail carrier as the ho-hum event it is. They will remember people they regularly see, and will generally greet your old friends as their old friends. In many instances, this is a case of the dog reading you—figuring *If Mom's cool with this guy, then he's okay by me.* Some individual dogs tend more toward the extremes—either erring on the side of getting edgy when they see strangers or falling instantly in love with them. Most, though, strike a healthy balance and generally see the world as a place full of potential friends.

Energy

If sporting dogs sound too good to be true, if you're wondering if there's a catch, this is it. On the whole, these dogs are high octane, especially for the first few years of their lives. They were bred to trot cheerfully through woods and swamps for hours on end. They're supposed to have energy to burn, and in most cases, they do. Some dogs exhibit this in the form of the doggie equivalent of hyperactivity. Most will outgrow it, but for the first three years or so, it can make life with your sporting breed interesting on a good day and frustrating on a lesser one.

If your dog comes from a long line bred specifically for a

calmer temperament, then this may be less of a defining characteristic.

Affectionate

As partners who have been working side by side with their handlers for centuries—and often coming indoors with them at the end of the day to curl up by the fire or at the foot of the bed—the sporting breeds across the board bond closely to their families. Even the more reserved among these breeds, like the Weimaraner and the pointer, want to be close to you and love to be loved.

Water-centric

I have a friend whose Lab can entertain herself for hours at a time with a game that combines her two greatest loves: a tennis ball and a pool. The dog, Francine, lives in Florida, and eight months out of the year (sometimes more), you can find her strolling beside the deep end of the family's backyard pool, dropping a ball in the water, circling back to the stairs, and swimming out to get the ball. Repeat. Repeat. Repeat. Repeat. The only thing that makes this dog happier is if the kids are in there with her. If you have one of the breeds that was bred to work in water, you've undoubtedly noticed that these dogs don't require a struggle to get in the bath. Many hate to get out. The water dogs long ago internalized a love of all things wet—a necessity for working dogs who needed to wade, swim, and dive in rivers, lakes, ponds, and swamps to do their jobs in the field. As a result, these are dogs who will try to swim in puddles, who'll dock dive with abandon, and who love nothing more than staying cool in the pool. You can give your dog a lot of joy by accommodating her natural attraction to water instead of fighting it. I know a wet dog is a messy dog, so this is a gift you can offer when you have the time and energy to deal with it. Something as simple as a kiddie pool in the yard or an occasional trip to a city or state park with a lake will allow your dog to indulge one of her deepest and most hardwired instincts.

Behavior Challenges and Possible Solutions

Energy Overload

When a dog is bred for hunting, that means they have tons of energy. Without proper exercise, any dog in this group can (and probably will) develop behavior issues. One of these is destructiveness. Most sporting dogs are more than capable of demolishing a door, a couch, a rug, or your favorite shoes in record time. They are super strong, and they desperately need an outlet. Because most sporting breeds are also pretty big, even a case of the zoomies indoors has the potential to do damage.

Unless you got lucky with one of the minority of the dogs in this group who prefers to be a couch potato (these individuals exist, especially if your dog comes from a long line of dogs bred to be service dogs or companions rather than active hunters), you must budget a good sixty to ninety minutes each day to giving your dog the exercise he needs (or hiring a dog walker to help you get there).

The saving grace among sporting dogs is that many of them—even those who don't have "retriever" in their names—love to or can learn to fetch. This is an excellent built-in exercising system for your dog, one that mercifully doesn't require you to match him step for step.

Mouthiness

Thanks to their retrieving heritage, many sporting breeds seem powerless to resist the urge to put everything in their mouths. Most of them outgrow it, but some do not. I've known a spaniel who eats socks and a retriever who got caught casually snacking on the tiny light bulbs in a patio display. "What are you eating?" is a common and sometimes stressful question in the world of sporting breeds. The solution here is twofold. First, get your dog some great chew toys and make them interesting by engaging her with them. Second, be careful about what you leave lying around. You can't avoid every chewing incident, but you can prevent a lot of the common and dangerous ones with a little prevention.

Appetite Overdrive

This is a breed group full of good eaters. If counter surfing were a sport, the sporting dogs would undoubtedly be champions.

Many of these dogs simply never feel full, and their owners laugh out loud at the possibility of the kind of free-feeding that works so well with many other breed types. Many a Lab would "free-feed" its way through a forty-pound bag of food in an afternoon if you made it available. Since your dog may never say *Stop*, it's up to you to establish a healthy diet and target weight, and to keep your dog from straying too far from those goals.

The #1 Command

Just like their compadres the hounds, these dogs need to master the COME command until they are 100 percent. A sporting dog without a perfect recall can't truly participate in hunting, agility, or just exploring the world off leash with his owner.

Great Examples

Labrador Retriever

For thirty years, the Lab has been the most popular purebred dog in America. That doesn't account for unregistered dogs, and it doesn't factor in the countless Lab mixes who find homes in part because owners hope the Labrador temperament will shine through in any genetic mash-up it meets.

The breed's history likely begins in Newfoundland, with the ancient St. John's dog—a landrace breed that evolved surviving bitter winters, living in a coastal environment, and eventually serving as a helpmate for one of the region's most critical industries: fishing. Sailors came to the Canadian shores from all over Europe, and they never failed to be impressed with the local dogs—both the big, long-haired ones that would eventually become the Newfoundland breed, and their smaller, short-haired cousins that would become known as Labrador retrievers. Those same sailors were infatuated enough to invest in dogs to take home, ultimately bringing Labs to the British Isles. There, too, the strong, smart swimming and diving dogs who seemed capable of learning anything found new admirers, and before long there were breeding programs in England and Scotland. This is where Labs were fine-tuned to be hunters' companions and to reliably retrieve in water and on land.

The big question about these dogs, I think, is how they made the giant leap from being outstanding sporting animals to being the most popular pet breed. The answer has much to do with their steady, affectionate temperaments, but also with their wide appeal across almost every social and demographic divide. There's no group that hasn't been successfully infiltrated by the Lab. Singles and families, children and the elderly, men and women, rural and urban dwellers—we can all see ourselves with these dogs. We associate their presence with loyalty and affection, comfort and companionship.

Any time you have an extremely popular breed, there's a risk that overbreeding brings out behavioral and health problems. With millions of Labs and Lab mixes in the US alone, there is also a wider variety among individual dogs than within many other breeds. An "average" Lab might weigh in the neighborhood of 70 pounds, but it's not hard to find one who tops 100 or even 110. Likewise, some Labs seem to be born with one less gear than others, finding it easier to settle down and relax.

Whether Labs of different colors have different temperaments is the subject of much discussion, but the jury remains out on that. Interestingly, though, in one fairly large-scale study of the breed, the single biggest predictor of whether owners reported having behavior issues in Labs of any color was . . . drumroll please . . . how much exercise the dogs got. As the saying goes, *A tired dog is a happy dog.*

When it comes to training Labs and other breeds in the sporting group, a good tip is to practice whatever skill you're working on in different places and different times (and if appropriate with different people). Most dogs are smart enough to learn to associate a command with only a certain situation, whether at home, or in the yard, or on a walk. You need to mix up the scenario before they'll become truly reliable and consistent.

Pointer

In many ways this is the classic field dog (so much so that most people didn't bother distinguishing it as the English pointer. It was just *The* pointer). Its image is the one that jumps to mind when most of us picture a hunting dog. This is the lean, powerful, aristocratic-looking bird-seeking phenom who freezes in a field, juts his nose toward his prey, raises one paw, extends his tail out like a flag, and leans ahead, saying clear as day with his body language, *Over THERE!* In the modern age, these dogs are still one of the dominant field breeds—still out there earning their keep. In the past they hunted both game mammals and birds, but today we consider them very much bird specialists.

This is a breed that is secure, confident, and single-minded on the hunt. At home, that confidence carries over into a manner that's often a little more aloof than some of the more demonstrative sporting dogs (like cocker spaniels and golden retrievers). The pointer knows you love him and he loves you back. He doesn't need constant reassurance. These dogs are athletes far more than they're teddy bears, and they do best when treated with both kindness and respect.

Unlike some of the more versatile sporting breeds, the pointer generally does one job and does it extremely well. Many of them can be trained to retrieve, but they're not naturals at it, and they'd much rather focus on finding the next bird than on picking up the one they already discovered.

Historically pointers often worked in teams, and so they're usually dog friendly in addition to being able to get along with everyone in the human family. Like all the sporting breeds, these dogs—the granddaddies of this way of hunting—respond best to patient, positive training. Tough as they are, they're sensitive to criticism and may choose to tune out if they don't like your tone.

Even though this is no longer the most popular breed that points, it's a testament to the tradition of dogs who do this work.

Vizsla

Unlike most of the sporting dogs, the vizsla is an ancient breed, one of the oldest forms of pointer who can be found in some form in Hungarian history going back at least a thousand years. This was a royal dog of Hungary, and it carries itself with grace and confidence. A friend of mine has one of these dogs, and it possesses a rare combination of talents: she's a keenly intelligent working dog who also happens to be a great pet.

The dog, Aja, got her passport stamped from Slovakia to California when she aced a working-dog aptitude test. Her athleticism, stable temperament, steady nerves (not rattled by loud noises, mechanical equipment, or the presence of strangers) were all good signs. Equally important, her drive for toys and play rewards was not just interested but obsessive. All signs indicated that she was not just the pick of the litter but possibly a 1 in 1,000 candidate for bomb detection work. She almost sounded too good to be true.

You can't force a dog to scent work. You can only motivate them to learn it. That's part of why a percentage who undergo this training won't succeed. Others don't have the necessary focus. This isn't basic obedience or even an impressive party trick—it's a skill that requires the dog to put two and two together in ways that some just can't compute. Despite the challenges, Aja was a rock star during training. She quickly learned to detect a range of target odors and to seek them with a single command. When she's on a mission, watching her is honestly like watching a dog-shaped machine. She vibrates with excitement at the outset. She searches quickly and methodically—every surface, every corner, every crevice—all the while with her tail swinging like it's a propeller. I asked if she ever gets fatigued or distracted, because scent work is both intense and tiring, but the answer was a solid *No*.

For many dogs who learn demanding jobs and perform at the top of their game, there's no dialing down their drive after hours. As a result, they don't make good pets. They don't want to snuggle or play, watch TV or take a casual stroll around the yard. They are too tightly wound for anything but work and sleep. This is part of what makes them great at their jobs but hard to keep at home.

What makes Aja truly exceptional is that none of this applies to her. At the end of the day, she goes home, curls up on the couch, looks at her handler with love, and inches a little closer for a snuggle. When she's not at work, she's a member of the family.

Vizslas are pointers, but these lean, muscular, copper-colored dogs are more all-purpose than that. Like many European sporting breeds, they're capable of doing all three of the bird dog's main jobs: pointing, flushing, and retrieving.

More Sporting Breeds

Boykin Spaniel. In keeping with the proud hunting traditions of the South, this internationally recognized breed is South Carolina's own. While many of the dogs on this list have histories that date back to European royalty and gentry, this one has a sweet and uniquely American origin story. The first dog to factor into the breed was a small stray who got picked up on the street in Spartanburg. When the dog demonstrated high energy, a good nose, and a spirit of cooperation, the finder gave it to his hunting partner who had an interest in breeding—a guy named Whit Boykin.

Hunters in the region needed a retriever they could take out on waterways in small boats, and traditional water breeds like the Labs and Chesapeake took up too much space and accounted for too much weight to be practical. With this in mind, Boykin set out to breed a smaller but equally capable retriever. He began creating a mix that started with the little stray and ultimately incorporated Chesapeake Bay retrievers, cocker spaniels, and other sporting breeds. The result was the Boykin spaniel, an expert retriever that tops out at eighteen inches tall and forty pounds of heft.

These sweet, tenacious hunter/retrievers are a source of great pride for their home state. Not only are they the official state dog, but South Carolina also celebrates Boykin Spaniel Day each September 1. The dog even has an affectionate acronym: in the fashion world the letters LBD refer to a little black dress, but in Boykin country they're often used in reference to its beloved little brown dog.

Brittany. With its distinctive white-and-red coloring, the Brittany is an easily recognizable, beautiful breed. Originally bred in France, this was a dog that working and peasant families could afford to keep. A wealthy noble might have a dozen dogs or more at his disposal, but a French farmer with a family to provide for couldn't feed and care for a full kennel. As a result, the Brittany was bred to be an all-around excellent hunting dog rather than a premier performer in only pointing/setting, flushing, or retrieving. Even though these dogs traditionally had "spaniel" in their name, in the US they're generally considered a pointing dog and go by their single name.

Today the Brittany has a number of inherited all-purpose hunting traits that make it perfect for sporting competitions. They run, jump, and swim with seemingly inexhaustible energy and frequently win awards for their athletics. They're great companions for dedicated outdoor enthusiasts, competitive runners, and families with lots of members to share in the collective responsibility of exercising the dog. Unlike some dogs of the sporting group who start to mellow out while they're still relatively young, Brittanys typically maintain their high-energy attitudes for most of their lives. If you're meeting their exercise needs, they're deeply loyal, happy companions. If you're not, however, they can quickly become destructive. They are the only spaniels who point.

Chesapeake Bay Retriever. This is the oldest recognized retriever breed by the AKC, going all the way back to 1878. It's also typically the biggest and has a reputation as the toughest. These are strong, hearty dogs who were bred to work hard and embrace harsh conditions, including icy waters, without question or complaint.

Chessies have a serious work history that includes not just retrieving in and out of water but also being left to guard boats. Perhaps it's that guarding background that makes the breed a little rougher around the edges and a little less warm and fuzzy than many of their sporting breed cousins. They are intense and focused, athletic and smart. Among all the sporting breeds, they are perhaps the one who most requires an experienced and confident handler. In capable hands and a home where he's given a job to do and plenty of exercise, the Chesapeake is a deeply loyal, loving, intelligent breed.

Clumber Spaniel. This sweet and rather rare breed is likely what you get when you cross a big working spaniel with . . . Eeyore? Heavy, fluffy, and low-slung, with giant heads and faces etched with what always looks like worry, these dogs make a big impression at first sight. In keeping with their build, they were intended to work like tanks as field hunters, pushing through dense cover. Beneath all the bulk, these are generally cheerful, friendly, easygoing dogs—true gentle giants.

Cocker Spaniel / English Cocker Spaniel. Once upon a time the puppies in English springer spaniel litters were frequently separated by size. The big dogs would be trained to hunt large game birds like pheasants and grouse; small dogs were destined to hunt smaller birds, particularly the woodcock—which earned them the nickname *cockers*. In the beginning, these dogs at all sizes were still the same breed, but over time as they were bred spaniel to spaniel and cocker to cocker, their gene pools diverged into the dogs we know today.

Cocker spaniels of both the English and American varieties are among the smallest sporting breeds (the American version is a little smaller than the English), and for nonhunting pet owners, this can be a blessing. It's generally easier to exercise a dog who weighs thirty pounds to exhaustion than it is one who weighs twice as much (or more), and as a bonus cockers tend to be a little more mellow than some of the more intensely focused hunting breeds like the Chesapeake Bay retriever, the Weimaraner, and the German shorthaired pointer.

Like many other breeds before and since, cocker spaniels experienced the double-edged sword of fame after Disney's 1955 movie *Lady and the Tramp*. Lady was a cocker, and her sweet portrayal catapulted the breed to the most popular dog in America. Trying to meet demand, some breeders focused on making a buck rather than maintaining these dogs' sweet temperament, and for a while there were some very snippy cocker spaniels with a range of health problems. These days, though, most cockers and cocker mixes are affectionate, adorable dogs who make great companions and family pets. They do have significant exercise needs, but they don't share the intensity and desperate need for it of some of their fellow sporting breeds.

English Setter. These large, elegant-looking dogs are among the oldest sporting breeds, dating back in some form for roughly five hundred years. They predate hunting with guns and were once experts at guiding hunters with nets to birds, then "setting" in a low position so their handlers could throw out their nets and flush the birds into them.

English setters are typically a little more independent-minded than some family-focused sporting breeds. They bond closely to their people and are good with both children and adults, but they also like their alone time. Setters in general and English setters in particular have a reputation for being "soft" when it comes to training. In a nutshell, this just means they're sensitive to your tone and body language. You can put them off by being harsh or using punishment. They're eminently trainable, though, with rewards and positive reinforcement.

English Springer Spaniel / Welsh Springer Spaniel. The English springer spaniel is the breed from which most modern-day varieties are derived. These dogs are a little heavier and taller than their Welsh cousins, but in terms of temperament and personality, it's obvious they're a matched set.

Descended from the first spaniels, these dogs were bred for bird hunting. They specialized in driving birds out of cover so the hunter could shoot them out of the air, and then the dogs retrieved. The English springer is an "upland" worker, an expert in hunting large game birds like pheasant and grouse. They've also been called on to work waterfowl like ducks, but these dogs don't naturally love the water like Labs and Chesapeake Bays. These days, like many breeds in this group, the spaniels are hugely energetic dogs who love their humans and want to please. They enjoy training that tests them, such as agility training and other activities that can translate into competition. They're still popular choices as hunting companions, and they also train extremely well as narcotics and other kinds of law enforcement dogs.

Flat-Coated Retriever. This is Koda's breed, so I'm biased toward it as a favorite. At first glance, these dogs can look like their more famous golden retriever cousins in black coats. The breeds are similar, but they're not the same. Flat-coated retrievers typically have a mind of their own. Don't get me wrong, this is a dog that will adore you, but he doesn't need your constant attention or affection—and likely doesn't want it. Koda's also a perfect example of how this personality trait seeps into training. In a more malleable dog, I might have been able to curb that prey drive enough to help him be the service dog I wanted him to be. But he was and is confident in his personality—quirks and all.

Another big thing that distinguishes the flat-coated from some of the more mellow sporting dogs is his exercise needs. All of these breeds require heavy exercise in their first years so that you can both get through them with your sanity intact. There's a point around three years, though, where some dogs settle in and can be happy with thirty to sixty minutes of vigorous exercise each day. For a flat-coated retriever, though, this isn't going to cut it. This dog with an intensive work history needs a good ninety minutes of active time to maintain his physical and mental health.

German Shorthaired Pointer / German Wirehaired Pointer. In keeping with the reputation of German engineering, these two highly similar breeds were bred with performance in mind. They were never intended to perform just one of the big three sporting job tasks—they were designed to do all of them equally well. As a result, the GSP is the most popular breed of upland hunting dog.

Most all of the sporting dogs are sturdy and strong, thanks to the physical demands of the work they were bred to do. But this one in particular is a rugged dog, built for strength, endurance, and athleticism. These are true hunting dogs, and because they're so good at it, many of them are still used in the field. Unlike some sporting breeds that have mellowed over generations and perhaps decades of being primarily pets rather than hunters, the GSP absolutely needs a job to be well-adjusted and content. He doesn't have to hunt, but he's never going to be happy just sitting around.

Golden Retriever. When you see a thirty-five-pound pre-schooler walking a seventy-pound dog, there's a good chance the animal at the end of the leash is a golden retriever. Despite the fact that this is a sporting dog with a long and esteemed history of actually hunting, in many ways the golden is the poster child for this book—a breed that took everything that made it good at its job and managed to pivot and soften those skills to become treasured members of human families.

The beautiful dogs with big square heads, muscular frames, and long, flowing coats are as attractive on the inside as they are on the outside. For the most part, they are exceptionally friendly and loyal, knowing when to be gentle and when it's okay to get a little crazy. They're playful and so get along great with children; they're reliable and trainable and so make excellent service and therapy dogs, and they can adapt into almost any household that can handle their exercise needs and doesn't mind vast quantities of golden fur on clothes, floors, and furniture.

Before they were all-star pets, goldens were all-star retrievers. Bred in Scotland in the mid- to late 1800s, they were rugged water dogs who earned a reputation for being quick to learn and intuitive in understanding what was wanted of them.

Even though a small minority of these dogs still works in the field today, most of them don't. Where you might have found a golden working with a hunter fifty years ago, you're likely to find a Lab or another member of the sporting group today. As many of these dogs get further and further from their working roots, some interesting adaptations to their modern lives are cropping up. One that I'm seeing occasionally that once seemed impossible: as these dogs get out of the puppy stages, they're becoming pretty complacent—sometimes even borderline lazy. They like to sit in the sun, to lie on the couch, to ride in the car. And they're happy doing it. Ultimately, this may be the biggest pivot of all for what was once (and in many cases still is) a vigorous working dog.

Gordon Setter. The Scottish cousin of the Irish setters, the Gordon was bred to find and help flush out birds in rougher, less-forgiving terrain, and they adapted to the task. The Scottish hunters needed a sturdier dog, and the Gordon setter is the biggest and most heavily muscled dog in the setter group. A male Gordon setter will outweigh a male Irish setter by ten pounds on average. These large, durable setters were named for the fourth Duke of Gordon, who helped establish them as a single distinct breed in the early 1800s, but their origins are even older, going back to the 1600s. Despite being big, powerful dogs, Gordons have always been notoriously devoted family pets. These dogs have mostly escaped the fame some of the other dogs in the sporting breeds have found, but it's come at a cost, as their numbers are rapidly dwindling.

Irish Setter / Irish Red and White Setter. The Irish setter has been a common sight on the Emerald Isle for more than two hundred years and is a descendant of the now rare red and white setter. These are beautiful dogs whose looks conjure up images of tweed jackets, pipes, and polished rifles. In practice, they still do best as a country dog, because they need a ton of exercise and like to have room to roam. For the first three or four years of their lives, these dogs demand up to two hours a day of exercise—and not just leisurely strolls. They are silly, sometimes exuberant, and you need to ensure they master basic obedience skills because that excitement and good humor sometimes translates into a dog who doesn't seem to realize she's big and potentially destructive. As they settle into their adult selves, Irish setters typically become a little more calm and dignified. Overall, they are sweet, sensitive dogs who make great pets for families and individuals who can match their energy level.

Weimaraner. First bred in the 1800s in an attempt to create the ideal hunting dog, this is a dog that could easily blend into the hound group or the working group just as well as it meshes with the sporting dogs. Weimaraners started out as big-game hunters in Germany, with bloodlines that likely included bloodhound, Great Dane, and English pointer. Thanks to a well-rounded melting pot, these are dogs of many talents, exceptional in both form and function. They can track, point, flush, and retrieve with ease and versatility. They are generally fearless (no doubt a trait that goes back to their wolf- and bear-hunting past) and they're highly intelligent—capable of learning almost any task.

Weimaraners earned their nickname, the Grey Ghost, for multiple reasons, among them their uniform and ashy coloring, their quiet natures, their ability to hunt and track prey in total silence, and the fact that they tend to constantly shadow their owners.

Conclusion

The sporting group is made up mostly of social dogs possessing good temperaments. They respond well to training, and they're fully capable of learning the 7 Common Commands and more. Within this group, temperament and inherent characteristics like energy level and prey drive are strongly influenced by type—those bred to be service dogs or pets versus high-energy athletic hunters. Understanding this important aspect helps you to understand your dog.

FIERCE AND LOVABLE LAPDOGS: THE TOY GROUP

At this writing, it's been thirteen years since I brought my Chihuahua, Lulu, home from an LA shelter. It was supposed to be a temporary arrangement, but even after she was trained, Lulu kept failing out of forever homes. She didn't like kids, or other dogs, or most men. She had a lot of fear and a lot of defensive aggression. Time and again she ended up back with me, until I finally decided she must be meant to be my dog.

Lulu and I got along fine in the first years, but it would be a stretch to call that relationship a bond. I fed her, trained her, talked to her, offered treats, and provided a soft bed (which she seemed to like). She eyed me warily at first, then accepted my presence comfortably but at a distance. I only picked her up when absolutely necessary, because when I did she would freeze, clearly wanting none of that kind of attention. I'd been around dogs long enough to know there's no forcing affection, so I let her be—and she tolerated me.

I was okay with all of it. This was a dog who had been down a hard road. She needed a home, and she wasn't much trouble for me to keep. At the time, my other dog was my Jack Russell, Pepe—and he was plenty of dog to love and manage.

Four years after I got Lulu, my world shifted when Pepe became gravely ill. He had seemed invincible right up until he was fifteen years old, but the time came when the vibrant, joyful dog who had been such a huge part of my life was just suffering. I had the vet come to my house, knowing that saying goodbye and letting him go was a last kindness—one I owed him.

That afternoon I sat on the couch, put my head in my hands, and let the grief come. Lulu watched me, like she always did, but then something shifted. As I sat there bawling, she made her way onto the couch, scooted up beside me, and then nudged my elbow aside so she could crawl into my lap. There, she rested her head against my chest and started to howl. She was crying with me.

I always tell dog owners, especially ones with rescues, that you have to let the dog decide when to break through its barrier of distrust and fear. But I could never have predicted that it would be the day in my life when I most needed to feel the love of a lapdog that Lulu would choose to be one. For whatever reason—maybe because she was going to miss Pepe, too—that was the day she decided to love me.

Afterward, everything changed with us, because Lulu was ready to bond.

Dogs have a way of getting deep in our hearts, and *little* dogs—the ones we hold in our hands and carry, who curl up in the crooks of our arms, who live in a world of giants—they're experts at it. Once you love one you'll never be the same.

Toy-Size

When you have one of these little dogs, you realize just how much emotional support and connection they offer. It's a different dynamic from the one we have with big dogs. I look at my retriever, Koda, who's a strong, lean eighty pounds, and I love and respect him. I also know that even if he takes off running, he's going to be fine and he'll come back. No coyote is going to take that dog down, no owl's going to fly off with him, and heaven help the dognapper who tried to compel him to go anywhere against his will.

When it comes to Lulu, none of that applies. She puts on a show of being tough, but she's vulnerable in so many ways. She's like bait for a bird of prey. If she ever crossed paths with a coyote, she'd be done. She can barely jump off the couch without dislocating or breaking something. So I keep a close watch on her in the yard, I'd sooner sleep outside myself than subject her to it, and I bought her a little set of sofa stairs. It's basically my sworn duty to keep her out of harm's way.

Taking care of another creature, especially one who looks at you with open devotion and trust, triggers the same kinds of loving and protective emotions we feel for babies, toddlers, puppies, kittens—all the innocents.

I may be especially sensitive to this because I've had to witness the harsh consequences of what size difference means for dogs on the streets too many times. Big dogs can fight, they can cover more ground, they can find food, and their size gives them some instant standing in the hierarchy of a pack. Little dogs don't fare nearly as well. They're susceptible to temperature extremes, they go hungry, and they can't defend themselves.

Even the way we pet little dogs is different. When I show Koda affection, I smack his butt, rough up his fur, squeeze his face, and roll around on the floor wrestling him. When I show Lulu affection, I pick her up, nuzzle her neck, pet her gently. These two animals may be the same species, but they don't have the same needs, and they do not occupy the world in the same way.

An Ancient Purpose

The world is full of dogs continually making a transition from working partners to simply pets. Most of the jobs they once did to support families and societies are done another way now, with machines or chemicals. Some of those old jobs are no longer done at all. When it comes to many breeds in the toy group, things are different. Most of these dogs have been meeting a different kind of need for a very long time, sometimes since their inception. They've provided comfort, companionship, and emotional support. They've been the objects of love and affection. And they've softened the hard edges, even on some of the most resolute and powerful people in history—kings and queens, officers and soldiers, czars and emperors.

This purpose, perhaps more than any other in the world of dogs, is something that hasn't been replaced. There's no substitute for a living, breathing being who loves you and depends on you. In many ways, other breed groups are ever-so-slowly moving toward this same purpose as their jobs go away, but toy dogs have been doing this work for centuries.

In terms of ownership, toy dogs also offer something entirely unique. They don't take up too much space, and they don't demand the lion's share of your time. You don't have to rack your brain to figure out how to exercise them to exhaustion every day. Their physical capabilities don't outstrip yours by hours and miles like a big dog's do. These are pets that have been molded over thousands of years to fit seamlessly into our lives, and as a result we don't have to build our worlds around them.

Many of the dogs in this group make ideal pets for people who simply want a dog to love rather than one to fill a bigger role, like running partner, home protector, or child's playmate. In short, toy breeds—both ancient and modern—are the original and perpetual emotional support dogs. There are a lot of differences among these breeds, but they have that much in common.

Key Characteristics

Small Size

The toy breeds come from a wide variety of backgrounds, generally divided into dogs who can trace their roots back to working breeds and dogs who have always been pets above all else. The main characteristic they all have in common is the obvious one: they're all somewhere between the sizes of small, smaller, and downright tiny. The single most important thing anyone with an interest in these dogs needs to know (and anyone who is a competent owner already knows) is that despite their group name and their compact size, they are decidedly not toys. They're living, breathing, emotional, intelligent creatures. They have likes and dislikes, endearing and disconcerting characteristics, hangups, habits, and needs, just like any other kind or size of dog.

The consequences of not acknowledging this fact are huge and heartbreaking. I see them every day in the form of little purebred and mixed-breed dogs who wind up in shelters or on the streets because somebody wasn't bargaining on a pet that would require time and attention. "Toy" is just a reference to size, not to function.

Manageable Energy

Toy breeds are the one group for whom I don't spend much of my time explaining to frustrated owners that most of the problems they're calling me about can be eased by giving their dogs more exercise. I do occasionally encounter toy owners who've taken the couch potato thing a little too far with their dogs, but that's not their big issue. In a world full of dogs whose physical demands can be a massive drain on your time and energy (though their companionship is absolutely worth it), toy breeds are the big exception. For many of these dogs, daily, enthusiastic play sessions are enough. For others, routine short walks do the trick. They are suitable to living in the city or the country, in an apartment or a house, and with owners who are active and not-so-active.

A Small Circle of Devotion

A small dog's universe is usually pretty small, too—and its family is the center of it. Thanks to their history as companions, many of these breeds bond exceptionally closely with just one or two people. Some breeds, like the Chihuahua and Pomeranian, are often wary of strangers—though others like the Maltese or the Min Pin act as if they had never met one. Because of their vulnerabilities and the close emotional bonds they build, toy breeds are rarely outdoor dogs, and they're typically happiest in homes where someone's around to keep them company most of the time. They don't need 24/7 companionship, but many of them wouldn't mind it a bit.

Training Deficits

They're cute, they're small, they're sweet, and we love to spoil them. It's no wonder one trait many toy dogs share is a lack of obedience training. For most dogs in the toy group, there isn't any need to be militant about this. Life will go on and you and your dog will love one another regardless of whether she knows *all* the 7 Common Commands. But there's a huge difference between light training and no training at all, and that difference can determine whether a dog is a pleasure to live with or a frequent source of stress.

Pack Sensibility

Few dogs benefit more from making friends than the toy breeds, and many of them seem to know it. I see this all the time in the play yard at the ranch. When a group of dogs is playing, many of the big dogs go their own way or pair up with one partner after another. But it often looks like everybody under fifteen pounds got a memo to congregate together, to build a little playground pack. Part of it is probably that they enjoy each other's company—after all, they're very sociable creatures. But it's also likely that they instinctively know they're safer and stronger together. They're like Voltron, assembling all the small, stand-alone machines into one big, powerful one. I've seen a pack of six Chihuahuas form a coalition and bully a rottweiler until he tucked his nub of a tail and walked away in defeat. That said, you have to be vigilant watching little dogs who take on big dogs, because it does not always end well for them.

Plenty to Say

Many of the breeds in this group will frequently, fervently think they have something important to tell you. They are barky, sometimes to extremes. A lot of this goes back to breed history, when protectiveness was part of the job of a lapdog. Some of it also ties into being territorial. As I mentioned, small dogs typically have a small domain—but many of them take their duties to keep tabs on it seriously. They've got a strong sense of stranger danger and can be surprisingly good guard dogs.

Big Dogs in Small Packages

Some of the munchkins in this group are exactly as they seem—sweet, malleable, easygoing companions. Others, especially the ones who have some terrier DNA, can be tough guys. And a few, just as in the other groups, have enough deep-seated fierceness to get themselves into trouble. People always ask if I've been bit by a shark or a tiger or a snake. I've been bit by a lot of species, but in almost every case that bite lasted a fraction of a second and then it was over. One of the most memorable and persistent attacks, however, happened about a decade ago, and it was compliments of an enraged Pomeranian.

This was a dog who had a known aggression problem—one that had cost him his home more than once. When his third adoptive family found they couldn't tamp it down, they enlisted my help. In some cases, the best you can do with an aggressive dog is manage its circumstances, and this was one of those. Thankfully the dog was no bigger than a basketball, so he could be controlled more easily than a large dog.

The day it happened, I failed to manage him. I put the dog's food bowl down—something I usually do and walk away. But I was distracted and hovered for just a second. He lunged at me full force and latched onto my hand in the worst possible spot—the web of skin between my pinkie and ring finger. His teeth were nearly through, and instead of taking his bite to make a point and letting go, he clung to me, causing more pain than a tiny dog should be able to inflict. I couldn't get a grip on his jaw and couldn't unhinge him. I finally had to shake my hand to get him loose. That should have been the end of it, but instead he came diving back again, this time sinking his teeth into my pant leg and again refusing to let go.

So there I was in my kitchen with this little monster re-creating every cartoon dog attack ever, and I was having a hard time ending it—mostly because I didn't want to take any measures that could injure this angry little dog.

In the end it was Lulu to the rescue. My eight-pound Chihuahua came flying across the room, bit into the Pom's haunches, and started shaking him. In that instant, any concern I had for myself shifted to my dog. I tried to call her off, but she was too focused on her self-appointed mission of saving her six-foot-three, two-hundred-pound dad. It would've been funny, except I knew where it was going. When the inevitable happened—the Pom turning around to go after Lulu—it was game over. I might have let him latch onto me, but I was under no circumstances going to let him hurt her. He actually did latch on for a second, and that's when I swooped down, grabbed the scruff of his neck to pry him off her, and lifted him off the ground. Even then this was a dog with no OFF button. I had to adjust my grip where I was holding him around the chest and under his front legs, with him facing away from me to avoid another bite. For at least another ten minutes, he hung there in the air, snapping and snarling and trying his best to get his teeth back into my bloodied hand. I had such an awkward and tenuous grip on him that all I could do was wait him out.

When the Pom finally came to his senses, he was beyond exhausted. He wasn't mad anymore, and he wasn't hungry for that breakfast he was defending, either. I cleaned up my hand and sat on the couch, and this scrappy little bugger crawled, panting, into my lap and fell asleep.

This was a dog with a bit of a loose wire and definitely not one typical of the Pomeranian breed. He was also the ultimate example of just how fierce a toy breed can be. For that reason, I've never forgotten him.

Behavior Challenges and Possible Solutions

Underachieving

Over the years, I've encountered countless toy breed dogs in animal shelters with one thing in common besides their size: nobody ever took the time to train them. In many cases, these are classic cases of creatures more or less living up to expectations. If someone doesn't think their dog is smart or attentive enough or that it doesn't have the temperament for training, that person doesn't bother to put in the time. Big mistake. In many ways, this disservice hurts toy dogs everywhere, as they are presumed to be unruly because of the wayward few.

Does your toy breed dog have the capacity to do everything an on-its-game retriever working as a service dog can do? *Maybe*, and maybe not. There's a reason for this that has nothing to do with your dog's intelligence. Many of the toy breeds don't come from a history of work, and so it's not in their genetic code to learn easily or perform complex tasks without direction. And that's okay. Does it mean your dog can't be reliably house-trained and learn to comply with a few basic commands? Absolutely not. You just have to put in some consistent time and effort to make it happen. I always tell people these things are not a matter of one dog breed being more intelligent than another. It's just that one might be more trainable. Both breeds have the capacity, but they function a little differently, especially if one was bred solely for work and the other was bred to sit on a lap. Genetics drive behavior—they tell the brain how to function.

For large dogs, learning all of the 7 Common Commands is essential to keep them and the people around them safe. These are animals that can pull you clear off your feet on a wild walk, who can inadvertently knock down strangers with friendly jumps, who can inflict serious damage with a single bite, and who can terrify anybody with even the slightest fear of dogs with a bark. But when it comes to small dogs, it's okay to focus on the commands that matter the most: COME, SIT, and STAY are a great start. Many dogs will go on from there to learn the rest of the commands and more, but we've got to start somewhere, and basic manners is the place.

The trick in getting through to most of these dogs starts with working at their level. To do that, you can get on the floor, or you can raise the dog up to your level by putting him on a table. In professional training, we've got platforms for this, but a picnic table or stairway landing works just as well. There are a number of reasons this works. First, it puts you level with your dog, making it easier to capture and hold their attention. Second, it gives the dog fewer options—there's no running to a corner or behind the sofa from a tabletop. Third, it alleviates any stress that you looming can cause your dog. Many toy dogs are very sensitive to human body language, and getting them up to your level makes it easier to deal with you without being intimidated.

Another consideration for working with small dogs is attention span. Sometimes this is actually a matter of focus, and other times it's a lack of motivation. Tiny dogs have little bellies, and they'll quickly get full if you're training with treats. The best work-around is to train in short five- to ten-minute sessions and to only use pea-size food rewards.

Protective Fear and Aggression

There's no excuse for any dog biting a child, but if you're a ten-pound dog living in a big human world, there are certain things that are important to you for the sake of your own safety. High on the list is being able to rest assured the people around you aren't going to hurt you. What kind of reassurance do you need? Predictable movements are critical. A calm demeanor is helpful. Respect for your personal space is important. So when a small, noisy, unpredictable preschooler comes veering toward you, hands outstretched, sometimes you get scared and react poorly.

We don't hear about bites from small dogs as much as we do from big dogs, because the extent of the damage when a toy dog bites is usually minor. These are Band-Aid injuries, not life-threatening ones. Ask a veterinarian what breed most often bites, though, and odds are you won't get any large breed as the answer. Chihuahuas came in first in one poll. In another, it was the dachshund.

We all have to know our dogs, big or small, and what triggers them to fly off the handle. Some dogs, for example, just don't belong at the dog park. Some can't be allowed to greet strangers at the door. Some simply can't be trusted with kids. All of these things are manageable as long as you control your toy dog's environment.

A related issue here is one of handling. Remember what it was like when you were a kid and anybody who wanted to could pinch your cheek, tell you to smile, or put their arm around you? That's a way of life for many toy dogs, and, like kids (and creatures in general), some of them don't like it. There are dogs in this group, like the Maltese, Pekingese, and Cavalier King Charles spaniel, which are hundreds—if not thousands—of years into stellar careers in being held and coddled, and many of them are fine with being lifted, carried, and snuggled anytime.

Other breeds, though, especially those that have working roles in their histories (but were bred to be smaller and smaller until they "sized out" of their jobs), can be resistant, uncomfortable, or get snippy with being handled without warning by anyone but a beloved owner.

Big Dog Syndrome

As you know by now, some breeds seem determined to deny their size (lookin' at you, terriers), as if acting big might actually make it so. Chihuahuas, Pomeranians, Min Pins, among others, are dogs who may not hesitate to get in the face of a much bigger animal to tell it what's what. Lulu does it all the time, schooling newcomers at the ranch, even ones that are several times her size, about what belongs to her and who should get to the back of the line if they want a spot on the couch or in my lap.

This isn't a problem unless it turns into direct confrontation, and sometimes it does. What exacerbates the problem is the way owners react. When two big dogs get in a fight, we treat it like an emergency, breaking it up and doubling down on training. But when little dogs fight, most people brush it off, call it cute, or even laugh. We pick the dog up and that's the end of it. Even when we get bit, we tend to downplay it. In other words, we sometimes let these dogs get away with having terrible attitudes. This is not a bad thing for a dog trainer—honestly, dealing with scrappy little dogs who've been allowed to turn into tyrants could keep me in business 24/7. But this is a bad thing for both owners and dogs.

Some of these breeds—as you'll find out in a moment—no matter how small, have centuries of history of being treated like royalty, sometimes even like gods, in their pasts. A sense of entitlement in a noble's dog wasn't always seen as a bad thing. And for the dogs who are part terrier—there was never any question they were going to act like they were ten feet tall. It's in the terrier code. This is part of the genetic fabric of some dogs, and because of that you need to swiftly and firmly discourage it any time your dog instigates another animal. Better yet, stay one step ahead. I've seen the tragic outcomes of some little dogs picking fights with the wrong big ones. It's okay to let your dog indulge its big dog syndrome a little bit at home among familiar people and animals, but never allow him to test a stranger. Things can escalate far too fast.

Prey Drive

Prey drive is not commensurate with dog size. Some toy breeds have little to none of it, inherently trusting that food will come their way and not feeling the pull to chase anything that runs. But like the many small terriers who retain their wolfish killer instincts, there are plenty of toy-size dogs who'll not only chase but also potentially kill small animals like mice, voles, and even rats. I've known Pomeranians, Chihuahuas, and Yorkies that were expert mousers. I've even been called by owners who were completely freaked out about it ("My puppy is a killer?!"). Consider a strong prey drive a reminder of two things. First, a dog of any size is still a dog. Toy breeds may be easier to manage than their bigger cousins in the other groups, but deep down they've still got wolf DNA in their veins, and it's part of what defines their personalities. Second, if your toy dog has crittering roots and loves a good chase, you can give her that in the form of play. It's a win/win/win when any dog gets exercise and mental stimulation performing a task they were born to do.

Territorial Nature

Mike Herstik has several big dogs, and tells the story of looking out his kitchen window one morning to see the group of them playing in the yard with a one-of-these-things-is-not-like-the-others interloper: a tiny white Chihuahua who was barking up a storm and running up to each of them in turn. The big dogs—a collection of shepherds, Malinois, and a retriever—were being well-mannered, watching the little dog like they were trying to figure it out. Since even a moderately rough response could have hurt this dog who had wandered over from a neighbor's yard, Mike went out to collect it and take it home. The Chihuahua practically leaped into his arms, nestling up against him and shivering as if it had had a close call. Touched at how sweet the little guy was, Mike gave it a soothing pat, told it everything was going to be fine, and headed to the fence.

As he lowered the Chihuahua to the ground, it clung to him—right up until the moment its feet touched its home turf. At that point, it spun around and bit Mike's hand, not once, not twice, but three times.

Some thank you!

It would be easy to think this was a Dr. Jekyll / Mr. Hyde situation—that the dog just lost his mind for a minute—but the likely reason for the attack is a lot more logical. The only time that dog showed its temper was when Mike "trespassed" into his yard. The Chihuahua knew the bounds of its territory, and the instinct to guard that space couldn't even make an exception for a guy who was just doing the good deed of bringing him home.

The flip side of this story is that your small dog may not be able to take down an intruder, but there's a very good chance it would let you know if one came around. It doesn't always take a rottweiler or a mastiff when a little dog can raise an alarm just as well.

One interesting twist in small-dog territorial behavior is that most of it comes out of insecurity. It's a form of defensive aggression—one that often gets amped up when you put that little dog in your lap. Lots of owners perceive their little dogs' snippy behavior when they're being held as protectiveness (as in, *This is MY mama . . .*), but the more likely logic for most dogs is that they gain a giant dose of confidence when they're being held—enough to even bring out a few growls and barks.

Yappy

Small dogs are generally the barkiest ones out there (or at least they're tied with terriers). This is part of who they are and not something you can train away, but you can manage it with consistent and appropriate responses. First and foremost, never raise your voice when the dog barks. When you do, as far as they're concerned, you're just joining in. So meet barking with a calm, low tone. Second, since toy dogs are especially adept at using their barks to become tiny tyrants, never respond to barking by giving your dog anything—not attention, not a treat, not a spot on your lap or a ride in the car. Instead, ignore the barks and reward your dog when he stops and is quiet. You can also teach a NO or QUIET command with the help of a penny jar or a Shake & Break training tool (and I lay out the steps to do this in great detail in my first book, *Lucky Dog Lessons*). Remember, though, that toy dogs are yappy for a reason. Many of them were bred for the express purpose of sounding an alarm if somebody got near their person. This isn't a behavior that will go away quickly or easily.

The #1 Command

Take time to ensure that your toy-size dog has a reliable COME command to protect her. An equally valuable command for small breeds is DOWN. This one skill can help keep your dog safe and managed in any situation, preventing things like door dashing and making it easy for you to capture and manage your pup when you need it most.

Great Examples

Chihuahua

I have a bias toward these small dogs in part because they have big problems. Animal shelters in Southern California are overflowing with Chihuahuas and Chihuahua mixes. Almost all the toy breeds occasionally have members who are victims of expectation problems—basically the thing that happens when somebody who's really only equipped to handle the physical and emotional needs of a stuffed animal brings home a living, breathing one. But Chihuahuas get more than their fair share of this. Too often they're abandoned after having no socialization or training—which makes them difficult to place.

This is a terrible shame because the Chihuahua can be a terrific, loyal, loving breed. Yes, they sometimes have hard shells, and they are among the breeds that can exhibit big dog syndrome, but if you put in the effort to build trust and help these dogs learn basic manners, they can be amazing pets. Lulu, who gave me such a run for my money when I was trying to earn her trust, is a perfect example. Knowing her love wasn't on automatic, that I had to prove I was worthy of it, made it all the more special when she finally decided she was mine.

A lot of the Chihuahua breed's history remains a mystery, but we know these dogs and their predecessors in Mesoamerica were associated with the ancient Toltec people and then with the Aztecs. At times, Chihuahuas and their forebears have undergone a lot of changes of fortune, from being ascribed mythical and mystical powers, to living on the streets and on rural farms, to being sold for meat. This is a breed that's seen it all, and maybe that's part of why they seem to uniquely combine the entitled bearing of pampered lapdogs with scrappiness and drive.

Maltese

Even in a breed group where royal connections are often common ground, the Maltese stands out for having an exceptionally colorful and regal history. These dogs have been known by a number of different names, but if you go diving through history books and artworks, you'll find them all across the globe going back two thousand years or more. They sat on laps and were carried under the arms of everyone from emperors of Rome to queens of England and France to Marilyn Monroe and Elizabeth Taylor.

So the most important thing to know about these dogs is that they've had a couple of thousand years to get good at one thing—and that thing is being loving, docile lapdogs. I've worked with more than a hundred of these dogs, and every single one of them was an expert at it. I've stepped into kennels at animal shelters where Maltese and Maltese mixes sat waiting, and most of the time I've got no idea where they've been before or how they've been treated. You'd think some of them would be guarded, or even aggressive. But when I sit beside them to assess their temperaments, without fail these dogs meander over and lean in for a doggie hug. They want to be held. They want you to talk to them. In many cases, I can actually feel them relax as they get that human contact, and they go limp once they're on my lap or leaning against my chest. Just like a husky wants to run, a hound wants to chase, and a retriever wants to fetch, a Maltese wants to snuggle.

In many ways, this is the original emotional support animal.

What does it mean for owning and training one of these dogs? For starters, you're in luck: you likely won't have to teach a DOWN or a STAY, because your dog lives to do those things. Your dog likely has a gentle, even temperament. In fact, I frequently certify Maltese as therapy dogs (and they're great at it).

Maltese can be barky, just like most of their toy cousins, but all in all, this is one of the most simply agreeable breeds I know.

Papillon

Years ago I got hired by a Hollywood executive's family to "emergency" train a papillon who was terrorizing the household, particularly a housekeeper who was deathly afraid of dogs. The dog, aptly named Rogue, would get territorial in certain parts of the house, guarding a corner or a couch or a bed and not letting anybody get near. I was expecting to meet a pint-size tyrant in this dog, but instead, what I got after spending just an hour or so with him, was a peek inside the mind of a master manipulator. Maybe he knew a dog trainer when he saw one, or maybe he was responding to my calm vibe (which didn't project any of the fear he'd been able to rouse in the house), but Rogue did not attempt to bully me in any way—and he picked up a number of commands on his very first day. This dog was a learning machine, and it was clear that he was fully understanding what I wanted from him as I put him through his paces. He may have set some kind of toy dog speed-learning record when he mastered the SIT, STAY, DOWN, and COME commands in quick succession. He made it look easy and would have absolutely demolished any preconceived notions about small dogs not being trainable if anybody had been watching us work.

Of course, a dog being well-behaved for me and doing the same for his family are two different things. I knew I needed to work with his people (including the embattled housekeeper) to solve the problem. Three visits later, I arrived with high hopes. We had been making great progress; Rogue was smart and funny and totally engaged. I was sure he was on his way to being a good citizen.

I walked in through a side door and heard a loud voice in the kitchen. Rounding the corner, I caught my new little friend in the act. Rogue was puffed up, baring his teeth, and menacing the housekeeper with such enthusiasm she had backed herself into a corner and was calling for help. I gave a stern, low, "Hey" to the dog, and he whirled around to face me. In that instant, everything about his demeanor changed. His body relaxed, his mouth closed, his head (and those giant ears) tilted to one side, and he came trotting over as if to say, *"Brandon! Buddy!* Didn't expect to see you this morning!*"*

He was so busted.

What was happening in this household was a combination of factors, many of which are common with dogs of all sizes—and especially with the Rogues of the world. First of all, this dog was smart (he learned four commands in one training session!) but wasn't being challenged mentally—and boredom is always a recipe for trouble. Second, he was in tune, like most dogs, with the emotions in the room. He was picking up on the housekeeper's fear and panic, just like he'd picked up on my calm. Dogs are experts at reading people—not at what we're trying to project, but at what we're authentically feeling. They know all our tells, because they can literally smell our emotions. Third, Rogue was so damned cute he had never had to be obedient to anybody in his life. From the time he was just a few weeks old, everything he'd done had been perceived as adorable and rewarded with attention, treats, or both by his family. He had never learned any of the rules that make dogs good housemates. Lastly, there's the Napoleon factor. A lot of dogs, big and small, would have slipped into bad behaviors in Rogue's situation, but for him the opportunity to take command of a room likely had a strong pull.

Once I'd seen him in action, I was able to work directly with the household members who were struggling with Rogue's behavior, teaching them to calmly give the dog commands, to reward him when he was well-behaved, to ignore blatant appeals for attention and negative engagement, and to quickly shut down aggression with a firm tone and a little help from a penny-bottle shaker. I also "prescribed" two twenty-minute walks a day, to give this master manipulator a different outlet for his energy.

After that, Rogue became a manageable little guy.

The papillon is an interesting breed because it combines the same kind of old European nobility history as a Maltese or a Cavalier King Charles spaniel, but it remains a typically curious, athletic, energetic dog. You can find these dogs sprinkled into Renaissance portraits from all over Europe (their ears make them much more identifiable than some of the other popular breeds from that time), but for whatever reason, they're still sporty. This is a Ferrari of a dog—refined and historic on the outside, but with one powerful engine propelling it.

More Toy Breeds

Affenpinscher and *Brussels Griffon*. Collectively and unofficially, I like to think of these two breeds as the Wookie dogs. Those bushy, bearded faces and big, wide eyes are as distinctive as anything in the dog world. Both breeds originated in Belgium and were once working terriers. The Affenpinscher is the older breed, and his name translates from German to *monkey dog*. The Brussels griffon has a similar face and build, and he likely owes his differences to breeders adding pug and English toy spaniel into the genetic mix. They are very sweet and loving little dogs.

These breeds worked to keep rat populations in Brussels stables in check and eventually made their way to promotions as house pets (though they were still probably expected to earn their keep by killing vermin). Even though neither dog has *terrier* in its name today, both still retain a lot of the intelligence, energy, and attitude that once made them great at their jobs. Over time, they've evolved to equally have a pet side, and they're funny, attentive little dogs. You can train them to do just about anything—and giving them obedience tasks to do (and rewards for doing them) helps keep them from getting bored and into trouble.

Cavalier King Charles Spaniel. Life is good for the Cavalier—or at least it seems like it must be. How else can you explain the extreme trust and goodwill these dogs bring to everyone they meet and everything they encounter? If ever there was a mild-mannered breed, this is it.

Toy spaniels were all the rage in European courts from the 1400s through the 1800s, and dogs that looked like today's Cavalier were among the favorites. This is a breed that's almost always gentle and is happiest just hanging out with you. Cavaliers are very social dogs, and so one area where they sometimes don't do well is in being alone. This is a perfect example of a breed that might benefit from having a second dog in the home.

Chinese Crested. When you look at all the dog breeds and try to pick one that's the most physically distinct from its wolf ancestor, the Chinese crested likely gets the blue ribbon—or at least the hairless one does. These lean, wispy, giant-eared dogs, some hairless and some (the "Powderpuff" variety) with long hairlike coats, seem highly exotic, but the breed is believed to have once been a working dog, traveling on ships as ratters. Where exactly the breed originated is a mystery. They have "Chinese" in their name; many sources point to African origins for modern hairless dogs;

and tests show that cresteds share some genetics with the Mexican Xoloitzcuintli breed. Odds of this narrative getting sorted out anytime soon to anyone's satisfaction are slim.

In terms of temperament, these pups are typically most comfortable as indoor dogs. Many have a playful streak, but they're happy to spend much of their time lounging, snuggling, and even being groomed. They're affectionate and love to be loved. Like most toy breeds, they can be prone to defensive aggression.

Chinese cresteds have some unique health concerns, starting with the fact that most can't stand to be cold. They love to be toasty warm, but if they spend too much time in the sun, their sensitive skin can burn. The breed is genetically predisposed to both epilepsy and eye diseases.

Any toy breed can take extra effort and consistency to housebreak, but this breed in particular has a reputation for finding it difficult.

English Toy Spaniel. This breed has spaniel in the name, but one look at their round heads and short snouts tells you there's more to their heritage than being bird dogs of any size. This was a hugely popular breed in Europe in the 1500s and into the Victorian era, and they are sweet, well-mannered lapdogs (like their more popular cousin in this group, the Cavalier King Charles spaniel). The breed bears more than a passing resemblance to the Japanese Chin, and they also have a fairly quiet, calm temperament in common.

Havanese. Likely a second cousin to the Maltese by way of their shared ancestor the bichon frise, the Havanese has roots in Cuba going back over three centuries. These sweet little dogs with big, wide-set eyes and long, flowy coats seem to have always been bred as companions. It shows in their easy nature and their affectionate, trusting attitudes. At times in history, the fate of the Havanese has followed that of the Cuban people. Their origins are as pampered pets, but in times of political strife, like in the early 1960s, some unfortunate dogs were turned out into the streets, while others made their way to becoming penthouse residents in Miami.

These are highly trainable dogs who require only moderate exercise—one or two short walks a day or some energetic indoor playtime in bad weather.

Italian Greyhound. The Italian greyhound is the smallest sight hound, but despite its ties to one of the great athletes of the dog world, this is very much a lapdog. Like the standard greyhound, historically small greyhounds can be traced back thousands of years to ancient Egypt. It wasn't until the Renaissance that these dogs became associated with Italy and with Italian art.

This breed is a rare and special combination of strength and fragility. Yes, they're small, thin, prone to being cold, and quick to show their distaste for chilly or wet weather. But they're also athletes, capable of great speed. This is a fairly quiet breed for a toy dog, and one that's very sensitive. Some people call them "Velcro dogs" because they can be super clingy.

Dogs of this breed often have delicate bones, and they can be easily injured. Sweet as they are, this is another breed that can be difficult to housebreak. The fact that both the Italian greyhound and the Chinese crested share this trait may have something to do with how much both breeds despise having to be outside anytime it's cold or wet.

Japanese Chin. The Chin is one of a handful of dog breeds

that's often and deservedly described as catlike. They're typically observant, independent, graceful little dogs. They like to perch up high, so they're prone to climbing on the backs of furniture. These dogs are intelligent, but often challenging to train. Sweet as they are, they're just not that into obedience. Fortunately, they don't need much training beyond the basics, because they're calm and quiet by nature. If I had to pick one breed as the least vocal of the toy breeds, it would be the Chin.

The breed is at least a thousand years old, documented in Japan at that time, but there's a lot of disagreement about whether it originated there or arrived from China or Korea. Whatever their origins, it's clear in everything about these dogs that they were bred for companionship. They bond closely with their families but are wary of strangers. They love to snuggle in your lap (and will basically not accept being relegated to the floor). They can be silly and playful and well suited to apartment life.

Most of the time, the only thing these sweet dogs demand from their owners is attention and affection. They're happy to go along wherever you go, but most are not fans of being home alone.

Pekingese. A friend of mine had a Pekingese who was found abandoned in a rural lumberyard. The pup was only a few weeks old at the time, and she lived the rest of her life in a tiny town with no stoplights and a canine population made up mostly of hunting and guard dogs. And yet, like Cinderella, Lady seemed to know she was born to greatness. Everything about the way she carried herself, the way she befriended people, the way she walked with both head and tail as high and regal as they could go, said that she was exquisite and proud.

That regal bearing is the legacy of the Pekingese, even centuries removed from their history in ancient China. Traditional lore explained their origin in terms of myth and magic—how lions were shrunk down by Buddha to join the ranks of small creatures in the form of the Pekingese.

One thing that most conveys status is exclusivity, and these dogs were as exclusive as it gets in their original role. In ancient times, they could only be owned by royals, nobles, and monks. Plain old commoners were not only forbidden to have the breed but expected to bow to it when they encountered it. The penalty for stealing one of the little lion dogs was death.

This was an insular society, and for more than a thousand years their treasured dogs, believed to have protective powers, were rarely seen by the rest of the world.

That ended in 1860 during the Opium War. British soldiers stormed and looted the Imperial Summer Palace, and when they left, the five Pekingese dogs amid their spoils were returned to England and presented to Queen Victoria and two other noble families.

Today's Pekingese is still a quintessential lapdog—happily bonded with one family (or sometimes just one family member) and always wanting to be close to that person. They can be playful and silly, and they're typically quick to bark at strangers.

Pomeranian. There are dozens of spitz-type dogs, most of them sharing Nordic heritage and many with the telltale broad, thick coat; small, pointed ears; and tails that curlicue up over their back. Their numbers include breeds like the Akita, Samoyed, Alaskan malamute, Swedish and Finnish vallhunds, and the Chow Chow. And then there's the smallest of them all, the Pomeranian. This is one of the smallest toy breeds, topping out at around seven pounds, but it's a dog with a big personality.

Like Chihuahuas, Poms encapsulate a lot of spirit and personality in their little bodies. They can be sweet, sassy, silly, bossy, and not accepting of strangers, sometimes all in quick succession. They're usually playful with people, but sometimes they can be little spitfires around people they don't know.

Despite the fact that they're not much bigger than some rodents themselves, I've encountered a number of Poms who are expert mousers. And that's part of what's important about them. These are bright, active dogs at heart—animals who still retain some vestiges of the desire to work. They can do really well at obedience, at learning tricks, and at playing games. They need someplace positive to put their energy, and if you give it to them, they'll be happier and more manageable all the time.

Pug. As one of the flat-faced breeds that was revered in the Eastern World, pugs are believed to be among the oldest breeds, dating back to ancient Chinese emperors and eventually making their way around the globe on trade ships.

Today's pugs generally have wonderful temperaments and personalities. They snort and stare, and they wiggle their entire bodies when they're happy—because a wagging tail is not enough. Pugs are like pint-size clowns, always working for the laugh. When they're not playing, they're typically snoring (loudly) on the couch or your bed. Even though they've got bursts of enthusiasm, they're generally not super-energetic dogs—which creates a bit of a mixed blessing. Managed energy is good because pugs' brachycephalic respiratory systems (shortened because of their small skulls) don't lend themselves to heavy breathing from exercise. It's trouble because this is a dog who'll happily sit on your lap and eat half your popcorn (which you'll gladly share because he's so damned cute)—and next thing you know your sedentary little buddy is five or even ten pounds overweight.

Pugs are smart and trainable, but their pampered history means they most definitely respond best to positive-only training.

Shih Tzu. This was originally a Tibetan breed, one characterized by lovely little dogs with good manners and gentle, affectionate temperaments. Their origins date back to palaces and monasteries where they were prized for being entertaining, snuggly companions. Ask anybody who owns a shih tzu today about the breed, and you're likely to get not just a loving description but a photo essay to go along with it. This may be one of the closest dogs to an actual toy, in that it will typically sleep when you sleep, play when you play, run when you run, and let you nuzzle it, carry it, and even style its mane of long hair—almost always without complaint.

Shih tzus are generally social dogs that adore their families. I met one at a picnic a while back and played with it for a few minutes. The next time I looked over, this dog was getting scooped up by a teenager who was obviously meeting it for the first time. Among the breeds in the toy group, there are a lot of different ways to handle that situation—from barking to snarling, biting to licking, going limp or struggling to get away. This dog's face said it all. She relaxed her body against her admirer but she craned her head back to look at me, her eyes so wide with discomfort and fear that she looked like she was going to pop. That was her sole protest—just a look that said *Help*?

I asked if I could see her, set her back down where I had found her, and watched her scamper off to safety.

Toy Fox Terrier. If ego is the enemy, then this little breed is in big trouble. A true combination of terrier (from the smooth fox terriers that originated them) and toy (from the Chihuahuas and other small dogs that were used to help shrink their size), the toy fox terrier is a tiny vessel for a giant personality. Unlike many of the breeds in this group, their history isn't as a lapdog but as a working ratter, and it shows in their high energy and bravado. They're the kind of dog, like a Jack Russell, that might pick a fight with a dog ten times their size at the park, so they sometimes need to be protected from their own basic instincts.

Toy foxes tend to be smart, and they typically love attention. That combination makes them perfect trainees for both obedience and tricks. That's probably why they've been part of circus acts and street performances for more than a century. These are fun, Energizer-bunny dogs who make you laugh and who can learn anything.

Yorkshire Terrier. The Yorkie is one of the most popular and beloved toy breeds, and it's another breed with a true working past. The original Yorkshire terriers weren't quite as small as the ones we see today, but they were little by terrier standards, bred to hunt rats and mice in two specific types of workplaces—textile mills and mines. Their size meant these dogs could squeeze between machines and into tight corners and crevices to do their work.

Most of today's Yorkies don't do much ratting. They're companion dogs, through and through, but they retain their high energy and strong prey drive—something that can take owners by surprise.

Conclusion

The toy group consists of dogs that are well suited to be loving companions. They tend to be happiest when they're in physical contact with the people they love. They're able to learn basic obedience commands and sometimes even fun trick behaviors—and they are better pets and more agreeable citizens of the world when they do.

CHARMING OUTLIERS: THE NON-SPORTING GROUP

During any given week or month, the pack at my ranch changes. My own dogs form its core, but we have rescues and trainees coming in and staying anywhere from a few days to a few weeks all the time, shuffling and reshuffling the dynamics in this big and mostly cooperative social group. I've had dogs from almost every breed, plus countless recognizable mixed dogs and mystery mutts. From the non-sporting group, I've seen some of the silliest, cleverest, and most surprising individual animals. Odie was a rescued poodle who turned out to be an ideal emotional support dog; Hachi, a dirty, matted Lhasa apso from the pound who was a boundlessly happy and eager athlete once he was cleaned up; and Utah, a schipperke who had the chase instincts of a great hunter, but an utter lack of instinct to finish the job when luck brought him the chance to corner a mouse. When it comes to this group, what most makes them special is just how unique they are.

The non-sporting group is an extremely diverse group of dogs with varying sizes, histories, and personality traits. How'd they all end up together? When the American Kennel Club began in 1878, the original breeds were from what we know as the sporting group today: retrievers, spaniels, and setters. As more breeds were added from increasingly diverse backgrounds, the earliest classifications were simply "sporting" and "non-sporting." Over time, the AKC's groups got more defined and specific, but the non-sporting heading stuck. It became home to a variety of dogs who didn't quite fit the defining characteristics of any of the other groups. Sometimes these are dogs whose fates have changed over time, like the bulldog and the poodle—once working dogs who are bred solely as pets today. Others, like the Shiba Inu and the Chow Chow, are simply too distinctive to put in any of the traditional boxes.

I think the fact that each of these breeds is an original or an outlier in some way is part of their charm. Rather than presuming there's anything we can say about their histories and behavior characteristics as a group that truly applies (trust me, there isn't), let's look at some of the most popular and interesting breeds individually.

American Eskimo

The American Eskimo dog has no connection to the Inuit or other indigenous peoples who were once labeled "Eskimo." In fact, this dog breed was originally known as the German spitz. They were once employed as guard dogs for merchants and as multipurpose farm dogs, but by the nineteenth century they were primarily companion dogs (and occasionally street and circus performers). They had drifted a long way from their working origins.

So how does a distinctly German breed pick up a name like American Eskimo? It started around 1917 when the US entered World War I. In a thought process similar to the one that gave us "freedom fries" nearly a hundred years later, it happened when anything associated with Germany was having PR problems. With that in mind, the German spitz was renamed the American Eskimo dog after a kennel in . . . Ohio. In the century since that shift, the Eskie and the German spitz have diverged into two different breeds, but they still share a lot of basic traits, among them intelligence, a sociable nature, and eager personalities.

Like poodles, Eskies come in three sizes. Regardless of height and weight, they're beautiful, devoted, and usually affectionate dogs. Unlike some spitz breeds who can require extra time, dedication, and consistency to train, the American Eskimo is typically an eager learner. Like its distant cousins in this group, the schipperkes, they seem to like to perform. Some basic obedience and maybe some agility training are ideal ways to both help them burn energy and engage their intelligence so they don't develop behavior issues.

Bichon Frise

This may be the original fluffy white dog. The history of bichons and their genetic predecessors goes back at least as far as ancient Egypt. They've been sailors' sidekicks, kings' dogs, royal ladies' companions, crowd-pleasing organ-grinders' performers, and plain old family pets as their fortunes have risen and fallen. Through it all, this is a breed that's weathered its course changes with grace and good humor. Bichons remain energetic, cheerful dogs who are always looking for a friend and rarely looking for a fight. They're also natural performers, wanting to please and liking to be the focus of attention. For this reason, they're very trainable, capable of learning not just the 7 Common Commands but endless tricks and games. I've taught these dogs to pirouette, to offer their paws for handshakes, to run agility courses, and to work effectively as gentle, reassuring therapy dogs.

It would be easy to look at a bichon and think, *That's a lapdog*, but that assessment sells them short. They are companionable, and they do like to snuggle, but they've got too much energy and athleticism for that alone to be enough of a life. Giving a bichon something to do—whether it's obedience training, basic agility, playing hide-and-seek, working a food puzzle, or exploring new parks and paths together—will enrich its life.

One last note: like those of many of the little white dogs, a bichon's coat requires frequent attention (weekly at a minimum) or it'll become matted and knotted. These are not wash-and-go, low-maintenance pups, and I've seen far too many of them in shelters with stinky, dirty, matted coats and hot spots on their skin to know this does matter. For the owner willing to put in the work, though, this is a sweet-natured breed that's consistently a wonderful pet.

Boston Terrier

Technically this breed falls among the bull terriers, but temperamentally it's in a class of its own. These dogs are goofy and sweet, loving and dependent. They're a breed that's especially adept at capturing your affection and never letting go. They form deep attachments, so much so that they often tail their owners from room to room. They can get pretty down in the dumps when left alone for extended periods of time—they're just very much people dogs.

Boston terriers carry the DNA of both bulldogs and terriers, but they've been bred for companionship above all else for more than a century, and it shows. They channel their energy into play at every opportunity, and they love to make you laugh. Any direct, playful engagement makes these dogs happy, especially if it's a game that helps them get some energy out.

Since they are a brachycephalic breed, they do best with a few short play sessions each day instead of a single long workout.

Bulldog

The predecessor of today's English bulldog, the Old English bulldog, was an athlete who had to earn its keep in one of history's ugliest sports—the terrorizing and torturing of bulls. The reasons for that now extinct breed's fitness are unfortunate, but there's no disputing that they were a powerful, agile breed— taller, leaner, faster, and with far more endurance than today's bulldog. The modern bulldog has been bred to be a better companion, but it's also been bred more and more for a highly impractical look. Many are so low, square, and heavy they can barely reproduce—and their offspring frequently have to be delivered with surgical assistance because their giant heads are too big to pass through a birth canal. Out in the world, these dogs are plagued by respiratory problems, hip problems, allergies, eye and ear woes, and a potentially life-threatening intolerance of heat. The now extinct OEB could have held its own for hours in a fight. Today's dog could have a heatstroke just going to the mailbox.

The bulldog is, in many ways, the poster child for what can go wrong when a breed is advanced for one or two aspects of its genetics with little regard for the others. In terms of temperament, this is a fantastic breed—typically sweet, loving, sensitive, good with kids, loyal, trainable, and relatively low energy. But he comes in a body many scientists and veterinary experts believe has become so impractical and unsustainable that the breed may never recover its health.

What does it all mean for the modern bulldog owner? You probably can't change the breed, but you can provide a loving, indoor family life for your dog. You can help it get regular, gentle exercise and feed a well-proportioned diet so that it doesn't put on weight (which is all too easy for this breed to do). You can pet and play with your dog and make it feel loved and safe. Compared with a lot of breeds, the bulldog is low maintenance at home. It's often only when the breed's veterinary needs start to add up that the people who love them begin to realize there is trouble brewing in bulldogs' adorable but impractical bodies.

Chinese Shar-Pei

I have a friend from China who was a devoted fan of the shar-pei, so much so that he'd owned several of them. He told me he was shocked the first time he saw an Americanized version of this dog, because it had a completely different look from the shar-pei of his homeland. Our version has been bred to be rounder and wrinklier—both traits that make them look appealing, but that also make this a less practical and ultimately less healthy dog. The long-held Chinese breed standard for the shar-pei reads like poetry, describing a head like a melon, ears like shells, a nose like a butterfly, legs like a dragon, and—my favorite—a face like a grandmother. I'm not sure whose grandmother the standard has in mind, but judging by the expressions of every shar-pei I've ever met, she must be a disapproving one. The entire breed standard is remarkably specific and visual—making the form these dogs take sound almost mythical.

The shar-pei is a truly ancient breed, going back roughly two thousand years, and its purposes have long been in protective and even aggressive roles. They've been hunters, guards, and fighters. The origin of their uniquely wrinkly and rough-textured skin was entirely functional. It was extremely tough for an adversary to puncture it in a fight, and its looseness allowed the dog to turn on an attacker—even while that attacker had a grip on him.

A couple of thousand years of selection for that kind of work doesn't yield a cuddly or submissive dog. Most shar-pei are independent, quiet, and appreciative of their own space. The breed tends to be dominant and can be territorial, so these dogs are generally not ideal pets for first-time owners, families with small children, or anybody who isn't comfortable being the alpha in the house and letting it be known. If you raise a shar-pei with good socialization and consistent training, for the right owner this can be a closely bonded and fiercely loyal dog. In return, the breed has an equally fiercely loyal league of owners.

Chow Chow

This is another ancient Chinese breed, one with a deep genetic connection to the shar-pei. Odds are that both breeds descended from the same original landrace dogs—something that, coat aside, would help explain the baseline similarities in both their appearance and temperament.

The Chow looks like a teddy bear, but that's not her temperament. These dogs are known for being devoted and loyal to their families, but they're a breed that appreciates personal space, and most don't care for being cuddled or snuggled. An upside of this is that Chows rarely experience separation issues. They can entertain themselves for hours without desperately missing companionship. When a Chow chooses to sit across the room rather than beside you (or trying to squeeze into your lap like a surprising number of large breeds will try to do), that's just an extension of that independent personality.

My experience is that it takes a little more work to get a sense of a Chow in training than many other breeds. Some dogs constantly exhibit their thoughts and emotions through their body language, but Chows tend to play it closer to the vest. You have to learn to "read" a Chow over time. Once you do, they still aren't what I'd describe as easy to train, but they are capable, especially with treat rewards in the mix.

Most adult Chows tend to have serious dispositions, and they're often described as dignified or aloof. That reticence, combined with the fact that a lot of Chows have a dominant streak, means owners need to be firm and consistent with them.

Dalmatian

Instantly recognizable thanks to their distinctive coats and the publicity magic of Walt Disney, the Dalmatian stands out in any group. Unfortunately, because of the fictional representation that these are cute, cuddly, docile dogs, Dalmatians often end up in homes where they're not a great fit.

The original source of this breed is disputed, but by the 1600s they were widely bred as coach dogs. Dalmatians accompanied horse-drawn carriages on journeys and kept watch over the horses. They were a beautiful, stylish, and protective addition to any road crew. By day, the dogs spent much of their time running alongside and out ahead of the horses, keeping strangers and stray dogs at bay. At night they slept with the horses, guarding them and helping keep them calm with their presence. Later they also famously worked alongside firefighters on their horse-drawn carriages, doing the same job. For this visible and important role, Dalmatians were bred to be handsome, strong, independent, protective, and most of all endowed with a bottomless well of energy to keep up the pace.

People don't rely on horse-drawn travel much these days, and the breed has effectively been out of a job (except for that of mascot) long enough to no longer be considered a working dog. They still retain the extremely high energy levels and guardedness they needed to do their jobs, but they don't have anywhere to put either instinct.

Living with a Dalmatian is a commitment in many ways—in terms of exercise, training (which is often slow going), and supervision, because some dogs from this unique breed have quick tempers. The best thing owners can do is give them a bare minimum of an hour of vigorous exercise each day, but for many of these dogs that's just a warm-up.

French Bulldog

Like its cousin the Boston terrier, the Frenchie is a cute comedian and can be a loving pet. I'll get a lot of pushback about this, but this is also one of the breeds I encounter most often because its owners are facing behavior problems. Frenchies can be stubborn, they are not what I would describe as biddable, and a lot of them try to hump absolutely everything that crosses their path (a problem that's easily solved by neutering). They are also prone to a wide range of health problems.

These dogs are adorable on television, and that's part of the problem. First, they've been bred largely on aesthetics with not enough attention paid to sound health. Second, their fame has made them so in-demand that disreputable breeders are falling all over themselves to get in on the fad.

The fact is, I can find something to love in absolutely any dog. I look at every one and see potential. With this breed, it's easy. They are lovable and sweet and silly. But after working with scores of them here in California over the past decade, I think it's only fair to remind everyone enamored of the breed that they are sometimes challenging dogs to try to train—so much more so than the cute and seemingly cooperative props they play on TV.

Keeshond

I have a theory about dogs with histories of working on boats— basically that since sailors and fishermen were going to be in close quarters with these animals, they took extra pains to choose dogs with agreeable temperaments. The keeshond is a Dutch member of the spitz-type dog breeds (heavily represented in the non-sporting group). It was developed as a boat dog in Holland, likely since the 1600s. The breed looks like a mash-up between a wolf and a teddy bear, and in the case of these dogs the teddy bear side is reflected in their personalities far more than the wolf. These are dogs with a propensity for both "smiling" and "talking" (it sounds like the canine equivalent of muttering)—a combination that's sometimes misconstrued as aggression but almost never is. In fact, I've yet to meet a bad-natured keeshond. Instead, the breed is overwhelmingly calm and affectionate, and is one of the most trainable breeds in this group.

The keeshond is an active breed that needs daily exercise and mental engagement, but it is neither a dog that'll lose its mind if it misses one walk nor one that's likely to tear up the house when it's bored. In some ways, the breed is a well-kept secret of the dog world—which may help explain why the kinds of health and temperament problems that occur when a breed's popularity explodes haven't happened to it. If you're wondering why this breed gets gold stars in so many categories when a lot of others do not, consider that this is a dog bred to live unobtrusively in tight quarters, to be polite, quiet, helpful, and tidy. It was not bred to hunt, fight, herd, dig, or run for dozens of miles a day. We've looked at so many breeds that go through their lives at the mercy of instincts that don't mesh well with the reality of being house pets. For this dog, none of that applies. They can basically keep doing what they've been doing for centuries and fit in perfectly well with twenty-first-century life.

Lhasa Apso

This is one of several breeds with Tibetan roots in the non-sporting group (including the Tibetan spaniel and the Tibetan terrier). There's almost nothing cuter than a Lhasa, but I get a surprising number of calls from owners who have found that they can be aggressive, up to and including being biters.

Here's the thing about this breed versus others that may look similar (like the Pekingese or the Shih Tzu): they were bred to be guard dogs, not lapdogs. Any hard edge in their temperament likely goes back to their thousand-plus-year history, where they were indoor monastery sentinels (outside, Tibetan mastiffs held the job). With that in mind, it's only natural they'd be independent-minded and wary of strangers. They were believed to be little lion dogs, and the description of a breed that's small but forceful suits them perfectly.

Even with their history being a factor, Lhasas can be great pets if they're socialized, given obedience training, and get regular exercise. They're also just as happy in an apartment as they are in a house with a yard.

Poodle

I've worked with poodles for what feels like a lifetime in a lot of different capacities—everything from performing dogs to Beverly Hills show dogs to rescued purebreds and poodle mixes from animal shelters. I've encountered them in all sizes and at all ages. I can honestly say that across the board I've had phenomenal experiences with these dogs.

My clients seem to feel that way. I know a lot of lifelong "poodle people"—folks who are so devoted to the breed they wouldn't consider anything else. This has given me the opportunity to sometimes train multiple dogs for the same families.

Why am I a fan? For starters, they are so intelligent. If there were a doggie Mensa, many poodles would make the cut. They're typically funny, cheerful, devoted dogs. In general, they have adaptable personalities, and that makes them able to fit into a lot of different lifestyles. The nonnegotiable in all of this is that they need a great deal of exercise (with standard poodles requiring the most). Without it, they can become destructive in their efforts to burn off their excess energy.

You don't have to delve all that far into the poodle's history to figure out the roots of these characteristics. They were originally bred as sporting dogs in Germany, and they were experts at retrieving waterfowl (their name comes from the German word *pudel*, which translates to "puddle"). It's likely this history of having the same job description that gave us smart, people-pleasing breeds like Labrador and golden retrievers explains why poodles typically make excellent pets. Accounting for the fact that they've been bred largely to be great companions in recent decades takes them the rest of the way.

One behavioral quirk I've noticed with a lot of poodles that can be a challenge is that they can't take pressure. I see it all the time in training, when a dog is doing great work, but just as soon as it starts firing on all cylinders and really making fast progress, it gets overwhelmed and checks out. You can almost see a switch turning off behind their eyes—one minute they're with you, and the next, they're done. Fortunately, there's an easy solution for this issue, and that's micro-sessions. In a circumstance where I might do a fifteen- to twenty-minute session with another breed, I shoot for five targeted minutes with a poodle. Then we hang out, or go to the play yard, or I work with another dog. After an hour, the dog is fresh and ready for another five-minute session. I can do several of these over the course of a day and get far better results than I can get with one or two longer sessions.

Schipperke

These dogs who look like little black foxes have a lot of power packed into their small frames. They're stronger, smarter, and fiercer than first impressions suggest. If I had to sum them up in a single word, I'd go with *intense*.

I like working with this breed because they're full of personality and can learn just about anything. I trained a schipperke named Utah who mastered the DOWN with such speed and precision he could have done it competitively. This breed's combination of cleverness, confidence, and independence is endearing, but it can also be problematic for inexperienced owners. If this dog doesn't feel like you're doing a suitable job of leading the pack, she'll definitely take charge.

The schipperke's high energy, confidence, and assertive nature go back to the breed's purpose. From Dutch and its sister language Flemish, *schip* translates to "ship," and the schipperke was an active working dog on barges and canal boats in Belgium (and also a popular shop dog for merchants on land). The characteristics that made this dog a desirable worker were a lot of power packed into a small frame, fearlessness in defending its territory, and the intelligence to be able to work with little direction. I'm sure it didn't hurt that schipperkes typically have big, eager personalities.

This is a dog that lives its best life as a companion to a confident, energetic owner. It's a breed that needs plenty of exercise, regular reminders that the household already has a captain, and opportunities to play.

Shiba Inu

If we talk about breeds that have one foot in the wild, the Shiba is definitely up there. In terms of personality and even lifestyle, these dogs are a lot like cats. They've got a feline disposition. Anybody who owns one can confirm this is a whole different variety of dog from almost anything else. They're cautious and observant. I've had more than one size me up during training, come close, and look me in the eye—clearly making some mystery assessment I'd never understand.

These are beautiful dogs bred to look like foxes—an ancient breed that's beloved all over the world, most of all in its native Japan, where it's the national dog.

As appealing as it is for its unique look and temperament, the Shiba can be difficult to train. Best I can tell, it comes down to a lack of motivation to cooperate—they're essentially lacking the genetic piece of most dog breeds that makes them biddable. This is so much the case that I've actually had calls from Shiba owners who thought their dogs were deaf. There was nothing wrong with the animals' hearing—they just chose not to react.

Conclusion

Non-sporting dogs are a diverse group of individual breeds so unique they don't fit in anywhere else. They range from highly trainable dogs like the poodle to ornamental breeds like the Shiba Inu, with a full spectrum of physical and mental characteristics in between. There's very little these breeds have in common as a group, but their individual histories are a fascinating peek into how dogs have been molded and shaped by selective breeding from the earliest days of domestication right up until today.

CONCLUSION

It's no overstatement to say that without dogs, people would live in an entirely different civilization. Through a combination of gradual domestication and deliberate breeding, dogs helped us establish permanent homes, develop successful farming and hunting practices, create reliable defenses, expand our territories, and communicate with one another. While they were evolving and becoming specialized at countless jobs that helped us, they were also becoming part of our families. We learned to rely on them, and in turn they learned to rely on us. We formed a kind of partnership, an unspoken pact to take care of each other.

In many ways, they are our oldest ally.

Part of the reason I wanted to write this book is because I'm too often witness to the breaking of that pact. I see the dogs who are abandoned at shelters or turned loose in the desert; dogs who've been neglected or abused. These are animals who've had to dig deep into their genetic code to stay alive by hunting and scavenging, by digging dens, by concealing themselves in the day, and seeking safe sustenance at night. I've seen dogs who form small packs to make it work, and dogs who go into lone-wolf mode, trying to steer clear of everyone and everything.

When push comes to shove, they can do it, can survive—at least for a while.

But the truth comes out when I take these animals out of the shelter or capture them in the desert or off the streets or from some abandoned building in LA. Dogs like Ashi, an injured husky I trapped in the brutally hot California desert; or Kala, an abandoned German shepherd scavenging around the fringes of a small town and trying to stay alive. Sure, they were surviving. They did what they had to do. They were descended from wolves, and they drew on the basest instincts they inherited from their ancestors and the resourcefulness of centuries of evolution and breeding to get by. But they were also terrified. They were skinny and dirty, covered in bugs and burrs, scratches and mats. They looked at me like the walking wounded, not knowing what to think of me, or what terrible thing might happen next.

Here's the thing about the nature of our relationship, though: each of these dogs took treats from my hand and let me put a collar on them within hours of their capture. Each sat willingly for a veterinary visit. Each tolerated a bath and a brushing. Each of them happily (if cautiously) came into my home, and each hopped up on the couch when invited, scooted next to me, and curled up close. These dogs wanted to trust so badly that, like almost all the dogs I rescue, they took a chance and did it.

Ashi slept for days, just grateful for a safe place to rest and heal. Kala bounced and played in the yard with a ball and all the dogs in the pack, joyful to have found friends and fun. Each of these dogs went to a forever home with a family, a bed of their own, a reliable meal schedule, treats, time to play and sleep, and all the worries of their gritty, desperate survival days in the past.

People betrayed these dogs, and I'll never know exactly why. But if there's any role I can play in ensuring any other dog avoids the kind of hardship they faced, that's the role I want to play. My hope is simply that this book will build a little more understanding, give readers a little more patience, and help strengthen human-dog relationships. I hope it'll help us fulfill our end of the pact we made millennia ago, back when we were just trying to survive on this earth, and they were wolves.

ACKNOWLEDGMENTS

Putting together a book is kind of like assembling a thousand-piece puzzle—without any picture to use as a reference. So many ideas, so much information, so many stories—and you want them all to draw readers in and help them embrace your message. In this case, the message was one close to my heart: that understanding may be the single most important component of a peaceful, happy pack. Time and again I've seen owners who learn the stories of their dogs bring their relationships to new levels.

As I send this project into the world, I've got a lot of people to thank. If you're reading these pages, thanks most of all to you for inviting me and my advice into your home. In addition, my gratitude to:

My Uncle Brian, for teaching me the art of animal training when I was just a child.

Jeff Kurr, for believing in my abilities when I was a struggling trainer.

My sister Kirstin, for always pushing me to be the best version of myself.

My mother, for bringing me into this world.

My beautiful wife Jessica, for being the best thing that's ever happened to me.

The team who worked at my side to see this book through from start to finish: agent Jeff Kleinman at Folio Literary Management, writing partner Jana Murphy, and editor Sydney Rogers.

The outstanding HarperOne team, including Laina Adler, Gideon Weil, Yvonne Chan, Lisa Zuniga, and Adrian Morgan.

My friend and mentor Mike Herstik, who committed to his role as a consulting expert on every level and raised the bar for the whole project.

Lastly, to all the dogs who've come and gone in my life: You made me, and I owe you.

Appendix A

THE 7 COMMON COMMANDS

There are countless commands you can teach (or try to teach) a dog, but there are a few that are all you need to keep them safe and make them well-mannered. These 7 Common Commands are the ones I teach every rescue dog I work with. Think of them as the ABCs of obedience.

For detailed explanations, step-by-step instructions, tips for working through challenges, and even photos of techniques in action, be sure to pick up a copy of my first book, *Lucky Dog Lessons*.

- SIT: This is the starter command for every dog. Why? Because all dogs sit. You're not reinventing the wheel or instilling a new concept in your dog with this one. You're simply helping them make an association between your command and something that comes naturally. SIT is also a gateway to other commands because it introduces your dog to the idea that they should take an action when you ask for it.
- STAY: The STAY gives you next-level control over your dog, especially in situations that might be dangerous.

Most dogs learn this one gradually—starting with a few seconds and working up to a few minutes.

- DOWN: The best way to appreciate the value of a reliable DOWN command is to think of it as taking the keys out of your dog's ignition. A SIT puts the dog on a quick pause. A STAY calls a halt. But a DOWN puts the dog in a physical position where it's a much bigger shift back into movement.

- COME: The COME command is the most important one for every single dog to learn. It's a powerful obedience tool, yes, but more importantly it's a critical safeguard for your dog's well-being. Every day in every city and suburb in America, somebody's dog runs away, somebody's dog gets hit by a car, somebody's dog gets into an unnecessary confrontation with another dog or with a person. Most of these headaches and heartaches are preventable if your dog has reliable recall—if they respond consistently and immediately to the COME command.

  ° This is also the command that takes the most effort to teach. There's no shortcut to doing it successfully—it has to be done as you condition, condition, condition your dog, until they eventually stop thinking about *whether* to respond and do it on autopilot.

- OFF: OFF does double duty in teaching dogs to have four feet on the ground. It's a way to curb overenergetic dogs who jump up on people, and it's a way to manage if and when your pup's allowed on the couch and the bed.

- NO: This is an all-purpose command, one any dog can learn with a little consistency and practice. So much of the NO boils down to tone and immediacy. Your dog should learn that when they hear this one, it simply means *Stop what you are doing right now*. Think of it as a reset button.
- HEEL: Teaching the HEEL is time consuming, but it's an investment in a dog's lifetime of fun, stress-less, and pain-free walks. It's an important command for any dog, but the bigger the dog, the more this one matters.

Appendix B

DOGGIE DNA: A TEST IS BETTER THAN A GUESS

Getting a new dog is the start of a life-changing adventure. If that dog is a mixed breed, chances are you're starting out with more questions than answers. You look at them and wonder, *Where have you been? How were you treated before we found each other?* And, of course, *What kind of dog are you, anyway?*

Some of those answers are destined to remain hidden, but over the past decade information about dogs' breed origins has gotten a lot easier to come by. Dog DNA testing is a big business that's here to stay as companies fine-tune their processes and build information databases with genetic information about millions of individual animals.

I know there are a lot of different—and strong—opinions about this testing and how it can be used and misused. There are HOAs out there using it to police people who don't pick up after their dogs, neighborhoods screening for breeds they don't like, and overzealous pet owners panicking about health conditions their dog might (but likely won't) develop one day based on their results. But those are the extremes. Most people, myself included, use the information gained with genetic testing to help us understand our dogs. We want to know them better, plain and simple. We want to get a glimpse into the biggest missing piece of their stories: breed history.

For as long as I've been training dogs, I've made sure owners know what kind of breed they have whenever that's possible, and I've helped them understand why it matters. I've copied pages from my faded old dog breed encyclopedia and handed them off to anyone who'd read them. I've used breed knowledge to understand dogs' motivations and to anticipate potential behavior challenges. This was my biggest motivation for writing this book—sharing the importance of breed history with a wide audience so we can all raise our training game.

In dealing with mixed breeds (something I do daily), for a long time I had to rely on whatever partial information or best guesses I could get my hands on. DNA testing has taken a lot of the speculation out of that. In fact, I typically ask my training clients with mixed-breed dogs to get their pets tested right at the start of our relationship. Armed with the information those tests provide, I'm able to better understand what drives each dog and what training methods might be the most effective.

People ask me all the time whether I think genetic testing for dogs is worth the investment. The answer is this: I'm always open to the adventure of training a mystery mutt. In fact, I thrive on it. But if there's a tool available that can help me better bond with and teach that animal, I'm going to use it. Genetic testing is one of those tools—a starting point for understanding the hidden chapters of each dog's story.